Sār

The
Essence
of Indian
Design

Sār

The Essence of Indian Design

Curated by Swapnaa Tamhane
and Rashmi Varma

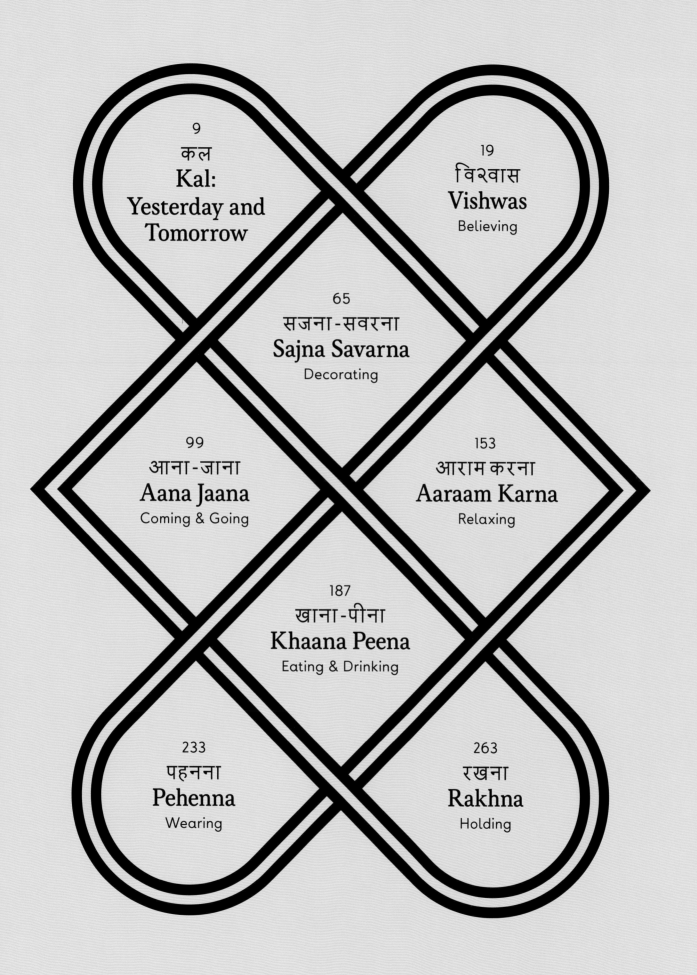

AFGHANISTAN

CHINA

JAMMU & KASHMIR

• Srinagar

Dharamsala •

HIMACHAL
PRADESH

• Shimla

PUNJAB

Ludhiana •

Dehradun

Chandigarh •

• UTTARAKHAND

HARYANA

• Moradabad

ARUNACHAL
PRADESH

New Delhi •
• Delhi

• Itanagar

Gurgaon •

NEPAL

SIKKIM

BHUTAN

• Khurja

PAKISTAN

ASSAM

RAJASTHAN

Jaipur •

• Agra

UTTAR PRADESH

NAGALAND

Guwahati •

• Lucknow

BIHAR

• Dimapur

MEGHALAYA

Jodhpur •

Varanasi •

• Patna

MANIPUR

BANGLADESH

• Bhuj

MADHYA PRADESH

JHARKHAND

• Murshidabad

TRIPURA

MIZORAM

• Bhopal

• Ahmedabad

Ranchi •

WEST BENGAL

MYANMAR
(BURMA)

GUJARAT

CHHATTISGARH

Kolkata •

• Raipur

MAHARASHTRA

ODISHA

• Mumbai

Puri •

• Pune

TELANGANA

• Visakhapatnam

• Hyderabad

KARNATAKA

GOA

ANDHRA
PRADESH

Channapatna •

Mysore •

• Bangalore

• Chennai

TAMIL NADU

• Thanjavur

KERALA

• Karaikudi

Alleppey •

SRI
LANKA

Kal: Yesterday and Tomorrow

We believe that the kitchen utensils sitting in our mothers' and grandmothers' cabinets inform our collective memories and have extended stories to tell us — and to tell others. For those in India and of the diaspora, the relationship with objects, recipes, ways of living or modes of dress is mediated through time and space; the stories that these objects tell can be communicated through their design.

A newfound energy in contemporary Indian design has permeated graphics, illustration, fashion and product design, fuelled by a new economy, and dare we say, a renewed pride in being 'Indian'. Contemporary designers are inspired by what surrounds them on the street, in the home — even on the dashboard of an autorickshaw — everything that, in totality, forms the collective memory and visual landscape of India. An awareness of these surroundings, combined with a new confidence to look inside the country for inspiration rather than outside it, has helped create what can be recognized as a new generation of designers. Against the background of a complicated history of economics and political manoeuvres, which continues to unfold, these designers are reconsidering the identity of Indian design.

Designers must consider how to encapsulate the influences and qualities from 5,000 years of history and combine it with sixty years of post-Independence to produce this identity. They must also consider that India is not a homogeneous monolith that can be fitted easily into one national congruity. Indian design is informed by certain objects, made from elemental materials such as stone or iron, that date back to the Indus Valley Civilization[1] and continue to exist alongside technological advances. In a country where one can see a bullock-drawn cart standing patiently at a traffic signal next to the latest imported car, there is an awareness of the coexistence of the past, the present, the rural and the urban. Creating an identity involves a contemplative dialogue about these coexisting aspects and between the sacred and the secular, the essential and the superfluous, the handmade and the machine-made, and the high-tech and the low-tech.

Sār: The Essence of Indian Design is a curated collection of everyday objects that reflects this complex identity and creates a platform for such dialogue. It is compiled from overlooked everyday items and a selection of contemporary pieces inspired by them. Some of the objects originate from outside India owing to economic and government policies and have since been appropriated into Indian society; others are influenced by external cultures in terms of their materials, use or techniques; but all tell a story of the nature of harmonious cultural synthesis. This cultural synthesis encompasses internal influences from many empires and dynasties — such as Maurya, Gupta, Pala, Chola and Vijayanagara, which collectively spanned a period between fourth century BC and sixteenth century AD — and religions, including Hinduism, Buddhism, Jainism and Sikhism. External influences — from the early Islamic sultanates, trade along the Silk Route, the Mughals and their Persian traditions, and the British, Portuguese and other Europeans — have also left distinct marks on the Indian design-scape. All the objects included are used daily and are, therefore, not obsolete or historical but very much present; we are showing them here in a non-linear way to demonstrate India's confluent culture and how its past continues to inform current design.

The selection reflects us — two Canadian women of Indian heritage who have spent much time travelling back and forth to India, gaining a certain insider-outsider perspective. With these dual backgrounds we have always been aware of how necessary certain items are: water had to be boiled on gas stoves for a mug-and-*balti* (page 282) bath due to frequent power cuts; hand fans (page 184) were used to keep cool; and Ambassador cars (page 102) used to transport large extended families. We have eaten delicious food with spices freshly hand-ground on a stone slab — the *sil batta* (page 218) — and lentils cooked in pressure cookers (page 218). During pre-Liberalization[2] we took with us from Canada the items that were not available. As we grew older we travelled extensively around the country, experiencing the nation's diversity, registering, noting and collecting what we saw. Our own works as artist and designer are informed by many of these objects, which teach us about ingenuity, materiality and beauty. Then, over the years, as Indian communities grew in the diaspora, we began to see a slow assimilation of popular Indian culture into the Western mainstream, including food, Bollywood, music, shops in neighbourhoods known as Little India selling a plethora of items from the 'motherland' — pressure cookers, masala boxes, jewellery, clothes, shoes and bindis. It is a culmination of these experiences and working in the contemporary design scene that has contributed to our understanding of what inherently constitutes design in India today.

The objects that fill these pages were selected from markets, museums, friends, colleagues and, sometimes, strangers in small villages who let us into their homes. In our collaboration with Prarthna Singh and the style of her poetic photography, we intended to create images with quiet, isolated perspectives that would distil objects to their very form, material, colour and use — their essence. A distinct visual language that would stand in deliberate contrast to the India portrayed as exotic, gaudy and loud. We are looking at these objects free of an ethnographic lens — beyond the vernacular, beyond tradition — and focusing on aesthetic values that draw from nature, geometry, colour, materiality, texture, simplicity and imperfections. To do so we have channelled the spirit and films of both Satyajit Ray (1921–92) and Mani Kaul (1944–2011) in order to celebrate a more timeless and minimal voice. We are not the first to elevate the everyday: these objects are icons of a culture that has inspired everything from contemporary art to literature. Artist Subodh Gupta (b. 1964) has used ordinary objects as conceptual metaphors by taking stainless-steel thalis and tumblers (page 226), tiffins (page 138), dish racks and utensils (page 294), and turning them into sculptural forms; Shilpa Chavan (b. 1974), creator of millinery label Little Shilpa, has created towering hats out of household items such as henna stencils (page 76) and *hawai chappals* (flip-flops, page 130). When one considers the multitude of techniques, skills, materials and knowledge used in Indian design that stand in opposition to globalization, there is immense value in these everyday, humble objects that do not voice their existence but have an inherent ingenuity.

Design is an implicit part of daily life although the word *design* does not exist in isolation in Hindi or in Sanskrit, because the artisan was considered a medium for the divine. As contemporary designer Divya Thakur (b. 1971) has proclaimed, design is 'an ingenious, spiritual, complex continuum' that has eliminated the redundant and assimilated the useful since time immemorial.[3] The *Shilpa Shastras* — the ancient Hindu science (*shastra*) of sixty-four arts and crafts (*shilpa*) — are a series of ancient Indian texts that expound exacting rules on how iconography, carpentry, textiles, jewellery and even painting should be produced. The purpose, reasoning behind and proportions of a craft object were considered predestined and perfection was a divine attainment. Many words refer to the design process: *iraada* (intention), *rachana* (composition), *banaanaa* (to make or fix), *banavat* (structure), *yojana* (plan), *namunaa* (sample) and *abhikalpana* (the making of something). *Sār* translates as 'essence' and we use it to reflect upon what might be the absolute essence — the rawness, the extract — represented by the shape and the use of these tactile and living objects. What is this *sār* that travels across mountains in the north and through jungles in the south; extends across both rural and urban environments; is shared by all classes and layers of society; and moves across continents, accompanying the large Indian diaspora? These objects are inextricably connected with a whole system of living — including walking, drinking, thinking, sitting, washing, moving, praying and holding. We have therefore divided the chapters of this book into use and action. *Khaana Peena* literally translates as 'eat drink' but represents much more: pleasure, enjoyment, preparation, sustenance and meeting friends. The chapter titled *Aana Jaana* (literally 'coming going') includes all objects related to engaging with the public environment, where so much activity happens.

In the process of researching and deciding which objects to include, we were aware that the handmade has been segregated as 'craft' and not necessarily considered as 'design'. A desire to consider the machine-made and the handmade on equal terms led us to learn about the role of crafts within the politics and economics of India. Artisans and their crafts, beyond beauty and skill, have had immense value throughout history, flourishing through the patronage of wealthy empires and kingdoms, serving the needs of religion and being an integral part of the village community.

In an unintentional concurrence between Hindu principles and colonialism, however, artisans were undervalued and their names went unrecorded. Art historian Ananda Coomaraswamy (1877–1947), who wrote about the encompassing religious perspective within Hinduism, said that the artisan was devoted to God through his work and that the Western concept of 'art for art's sake' was not relevant. This belief, that artisans were purely a medium for the Divine, served to eliminate their personal identity. Sir George Birdwood (1832–1917), who was born in India and later became keeper of the Indian Museum at South Kensington (now part of the collections at the Victoria and Albert Museum, London) idealized the artisan's life in his two volumes, *The Industrial Arts of India*, an incredibly detailed account of crafts throughout the country. The first volume speaks of religion — that being Hinduism — to explain the connections between craft and ritual. Although he was a crafts activist, his account does not include crafts or influences from other religions and thereby discounts, for example, great artistic and decorative art forms that were the result of an aesthetic harmony between differing Islamic and Hindu guidelines. Both Coomaraswamy and Birdwood linked Hinduism to an understanding of crafts — what they called 'industrial arts' — but did not consider everyday objects or link crafts to daily life.

Under colonialism, the artisan's devotion to the Divine through this work was negated by economic factors, as the colonialist businessman was interested only in logistics — where the craft was produced and how long it would take to transport it to commercial seaports. The artisan became a tool of mass-production for export rather than a transmitter for the Divine. A foreword to Coomaraswamy's *The Indian Craftsman* explains: 'As far as the ancient Indian craftsman was concerned, his way of the gods was destroyed, in part, by the advent of the Europeans […] And these men introduced free trade and free, i.e., cut-throat competition, and the unbridled lust for gain. But if the Europeans played the role of spoilers, the Indians themselves were not blameless; their own slackness and forgetfulness had, in effect, created a low pressure area which invited European interference.'[4] Expecting the artisan to make the same product over and over again was not a new concept solely introduced by the European hunger for productivity. The idea of change or individuality had never been encouraged within craft. As textile historian Jasleen Dhamija (b. 1933) writes: 'Handicrafts, defined simply, are objects made by the skill of the hand which carry a part of the creator as well as centuries of tradition in which they have been created.'[5] The potter (*kumhar*) proudly continues to make the same object inspired by ritual or tradition, often fulfilling a community's heritage. Art historian Vidya Dehejia (b. 1942) comments, too, that individuality was not encouraged as an aspect of creativity and that 'rather the repetition of an idealized formula was extolled and prized'.[6]

While the individual artisan often went unrecognized, the artisan as a symbol was used as a political pawn. The craftsperson — epitomized as the ideal martyr, leading a pure life, working quietly in a small village and self-sufficient — was presented as a nationalist metaphor at the heart of the anti-colonial movement by such figures as Mahatma Gandhi (1869–1948). Earlier, nineteenth-century social thinker and art critic John Ruskin and activist and textile designer William Morris, the latter greatly influenced by Indian aesthetics, saw the artisan as a form of resistance to modern industrialization and as a conduit for creating a voice for one's culture. So the innocent artisan was positioned in this conflicting way — both idealized and irrelevant — at a time in history that coincided with a series of events that also sparked the 'imperial gaze' on India aesthetically and conceptually — a gaze that prevails to this day.

London's Great Exhibition of 1851 showcased manufactured objects from Britain and its colonies, including crafts from India, to show off the techniques and resources that were in abundance. While craft objects were celebrated and held in awe, the machinery used to make them was sneered at and viewed as rudimentary.[7] This exhibition, held to encourage trade for items made to appeal to the West, was also, in part, motivated by wanting to provide new product ideas to reform British manufacturers. In India tensions were rising between the locals and the British Raj (1858–1947), which was suffocating and stamping out the development of many Indian industries — in particular, the textile industry, since it was in competition with Britain's own. Pashmina shawls (page 236), also known as the 'Kashmir' or 'paisley shawl', were in such great demand in Europe that British manufacturers soon industrialized their own looms to produce imitations in order to meet sartorial demands, and this proved detrimental to the Kashmiri weavers. The Mutiny of 1857 and the Indigo revolts in Bengal in 1859 were a clear indication of dissatisfaction with British rule, and so began the long fight for independence.

Further exhibitions to include Indian handicrafts (the Paris Universal Exhibition in 1878 and the Delhi Durbar Exhibition in 1903) took place alongside historical events that involved new concepts in education, namely the founding in 1901 of the Visva-Bharati University in Santiniketan by Rabindranath Tagore (1861–1941), where students studied fine arts, music, science and agriculture in lessons that were held in a natural environment. In 1922, Tagore hired the Viennese art historian Stella Kramrisch to teach

Indian art history, when she also organized the fourteenth Annual Exhibition of the Indian Society of Oriental Art in Calcutta (Kolkata), which brought together contemporary artists from Bengal and the Bauhaus, demonstrating a developing philosophy of the avant-garde, aesthetics and design. Exhibited paintings included those by Nandalal Bose (1882–1966) and Gaganendranath Tagore (1867–1938), alongside paintings and woodcuts by Johannes Itten, Auguste Macke and Wassily Kandinsky. Japanese-American architect and woodworker George Nakashima was very much influenced by the teachings of Indian nationalist Sri Aurobindo (1872–1950) and spent two years volunteering at his ashram in Pondicherry between 1937 and 1939, where he made his first furniture. It is no accident that such examples of global exchanges between artists and designers, and their consequent convergences, occurred simultaneously with desires for independence, and were motivated by a wish to find their own indigenous contemporary language.

Gandhi, who also spent time at Santiniketan, began physically to embody the ideal artisan as a metaphor of *swadeshi* (literally meaning 'one's own country', this was a nationalist movement that rejected British-made goods and promoted self-sufficiency by producing Indian-made goods). He made and wore his own clothes made out of *khadi* (cotton cloth) handspun on the charkha (spinning wheel, page 248). Contradictory to Gandhi's philosophy, Rabindranath Tagore had argued in 1917 that the idea of nationalism was socially difficult in a country composed of separate villages, languages and castes. Instead, he believed that various saints, such as the fifteenth-century poet and weaver Kabir, could unite all religions, and create a spiritual union for the benefit of the identity of the nation as a whole.[8] Both Gandhi and Tagore, even with their differing ideologies, influenced many artists and craft activists — and, indeed, continue to do so.

In the meantime, the vision of India's first Prime Minister, Jawaharlal Nehru (1889–1964), was to create an entirely self-sufficient industrial country. A supporter of Gandhi's Swadeshi movement, he tried to integrate craft and industrialization, recognizing that the artisan formed the economic backbone of the country. When India gained independence and Nehru took office in 1947, approximately one in thirty Indians were dependent on some sort of handicraft for their earnings;[9] thus to ignore the artisan would have been economically disastrous for the nation. Nehru was forced to introduce a mixed economy that could accommodate both the continuation

of cottage industries and new mechanization, while also melding the private and public sectors. He was intent on building the country up after Independence, particularly because India had the advantage of being unaffected by both world wars. He nationalized the steel, iron, coal and nuclear power industries while also focusing on agriculture and founding institutions of higher learning. He established the All India Handloom Board, appointing activist and writer Pupul Jayakar (1915–97) as its chair, her remit to study the current state of the handicrafts sector and how it might be revived. The Khadi and Village Industries Commission was also established in order to gather data and knowledge about craft clusters,[10] conditions of working and so on, there having previously been no such information in existence. The expertise and awareness fostered by these organizations has had a profound effect on dialogues and collaborations that take place between designers and the craft clusters today.

Jayakar also arranged for Nehru and the twentieth-century American architect-artist team Charles and Ray Eames to meet, after she had met them in 1955 at the Museum of Modern Art's *Textiles and Ornamental Arts of India* exhibition, of which the Eameses made a cinematic record. At the time of Independence there had been only around 300 trained Indian architects and, encouraged by his meeting with the Eameses, Nehru realized the need for 'a language of design', which could be developed at modern institutions and help further social progress. As the nation developed, those young designers and architects who could afford the expense went abroad to pursue their studies at institutions such as Harvard University or Massachusetts Institute of Technology and worked with architects such as Walter Gropius, Le Corbusier, Louis Kahn and Frank Lloyd Wright. Noted architects Charles Correa (1930–2015), Habib Rahman, (1915–95) Achyut Kanvinde (1916–2002) and Balkrishna Vithaldas Doshi (b. 1927) returned to India fresh and optimistic, brimming with ideas to design a new national architectural identity and lexicon. They created some of the most notable post-Independence architecture, which continues to inspire new generations of architects and designers today. In 1957 the Eameses were invited to tour India for three months, after which they delivered *The India Report*. They were asked to develop ideas around a programme of design training, which led to the inauguration of the National Institute of Design in Ahmedabad in 1961. They encouraged the creation of a national conscience through research, listing a broad range of courses that included engineering,

painting, theory, architecture, music and literature —
perhaps a synthesis of what Santiniketan and older
schools such as the Sir J.J. School of Art in Mumbai
had intended.

It was the Eameses, in *The India Report*, who
articulated that 'design' was an 'unselfconscious'
process, using the *lota* (water pot, page 294) as a
key illustration.[11] Cultural theorist and museologist
Jyotindra Jain (b. 1943) explains that the *lota* was
derived from nature — from a gourd, which would
have been used naturally before the use of metal
or even earthenware.[12] Crafts activist Kamaladevi
Chattopadhyay (1903–88), in her seminal book
Handicrafts of India, presents the *lota* as an
ahistorical symbol of divinity: it represents creation
during the epic Churning of the Ocean when the gods
extracted the nectar from the water, and celestial
artificer Vishwakarma created a pot into which to
place the liquid. A pot filled with water has often
been used to represent a deity during worship or a
ceremony.[13] The *lota* is an ideal example of an object
that is not designed by anyone in particular but is
'designed' anew everyday by anyone and everyone,
as the form of the object meets the form of the body,
fitting into the waist and held by the wrist or hand.
The Eameses recognized the *lota* as something that
could not be 'designed', being a form that 'arises
from the deeper hunger of humanity, its functions
socialized, for its use is distributed through the family
and the entire community'. If it were to be designed
it would be necessary to 'shut out all preconceived
ideas on the subject' in order to consider how it is
transported, how it is used, what it carries and so
forth. The unselfconscious object often results from
the overlapping of influences from pre-existing
technologies, when older traditions or techniques
are replaced by modified or new ones. Through
habit and use, the newer material is adapted to suit
the old form, plastic replacing metal, for instance.[14]

What the Eameses emphasize is that utensils or
objects of daily use — some of which had been in use
since early Indus Valley times, such as iron, stone or
wooden objects — display, as Jain succinctly explains,
'a remarkable degree of aesthetic awareness and
a tremendous sense of usability combined with
practicality and beauty'. Jain elucidates the process
of integration: 'These earlier and later elements have
not only survived side by side but have influenced one
another. It is interesting to note that, when an ancient
tradition of technology modernizes due to the advent
of new materials, there is a slow transition from the
old. The objects belonging to this period of transition
throw light on the creativity of the craftsmen. As they

impose pre-existing forms and technologies onto the
new material — creating transitional hybrid forms,
some of which are discarded over time, and others,
adapted and absorbed.'[15] Unselfconsciousness went
hand in hand with a non-preciousness that was easily
overlooked in a recently independent country that
was more focused on coming to terms with modernity.

Nevertheless, thanks partly to the Eameses, an
Indian design identity was forming and was given a
boost by the policies established by the Bandung
Conference, which took place in 1955 (coincidentally,
six days after the opening of *Textiles and Ornamental
Arts of India* exhibition). This was the historic meeting
of Asian and African states consolidating themselves
as the Non-Aligned Movement, whose aims were to
counteract the dominant power of the United States
and the Western and Eastern Blocs in the Cold War,
resist imperialism and colonialism, and also engage
in mutually beneficial trade. The conference ushered
in licensing deals from around the world, which helped
create a manufacturing market in India and explains
why certain 'foreign' objects are now ubiquitous in
India: scooters (page 110) and autorickshaws based on
models made by the Italian company Piaggio but
manufactured by local companies (page 130); the Fiat,
which became the iconic black-and-yellow Mumbai
taxi produced by Premier Automobiles (page 134);
and even the L.G. Hawkins pressure cooker (page
218). These are products that we have included in
Sār: The Essence of Indian Design to illustrate local
appropriation and adaptation to the extent of their
becoming representative of everyday life. Not to
include these objects because they originated outside
India would be to ignore their political and economic
context and dismiss how they were adapted and
merged into Indian life, thus becoming an inherent
part of India's material culture.

Licensing deals were not the only catalyst for
Indian design: special craft fairs were organized by
the government in order to reconnect urban Indians
to handmade objects and particular craft clusters
grew with the support of NGOs dedicated to
sustaining employment through craft. Individual
designers and patrons of art and design also began
to dedicate their efforts towards 'craft revival', like
fashion designer Ritu Kumar (b. 1944), or Maharani
Gayatri Devi (1919–2009) who, in the 1940s, funded
individuals to learn the art of Jaipur blue pottery.
Despite all these efforts, many artisans struggled
immensely through misguided policies, middlemen
and traders, and a generally low value of their
workmanship. As a result the artisans were further
marginalized and continued to live in poverty.

Even as late as 1984, artist and pedagogue K.G. Subramanyan (b. 1924) was asking whether hands have a chance given the impoverished mindset evident in national policies on the sustenance of handicrafts. Parallel to this, serious efforts continued on the part of designers, who posed similar questions on the global stage in order to build an awareness of the potential of Indian design. In 1985 a notable exhibition, bridging the gap between the past and present and between artisans and designers, was curator Rajeev Sethi's (b. 1949) *The Golden Eye: An International Tribute to the Artisans of India* at the Cooper Hewitt, Smithsonian Design Museum. Designers and architects from Europe and America, such as Ettore Sottsass, Hans Hollein, Frei Otto, Mary McFadden and Mario Bellini, collaborated with young Indian designers and artisans to create a collection of some 250 objects out of wood, stone and metal. In 1986 the Ministry of Textiles created the National Institute of Fashion Technology, India's first fashion school, and, in the decades to follow, the concept of the fashion designer would soon enter everyday language.

The winds of economic change brought about liberalization in India in the early 1990s, so that today capitalism and a free market are valued. Perhaps a symbol of this new era is the replacement of the traditional flowers making up the bridegroom's *haar* or *mala* (garland), with crisp 10 to 1,000 rupee notes, as obvious markers of wealth and success. Economic reform was developed by Dr Manmohan Singh (b. 1932), Minister of Finance from 1991–96 (and later Prime Minister), who decreased high import taxes and allowed foreign companies to enter the local market in order to sell and produce goods within the country, and broke up monopolies, creating a competitive marketplace that would give consumers an abundance of choice.

This new open market has created fertile ground for contemporary designers and the mass-production of goods to match changes in lifestyle that are more aspirational and consumer-driven. Design is now, sixty years after Independence, forming a national identity and its own lexicon — free of religious boundaries, informed by the mainstream and pop culture, while also being aware of historical influences. Attention given by contemporary designers to the abundance of craft clusters, existing technologies, materials and resources with which to make a new language of design culture is now taking place. This idea of seeing and valuing that which surrounds them that is interesting, clever, beautiful and utterly 'Indian' has — for the many reasons explained here — taken time.

In order to determine in what directions they should take Indian design, designers are faced with the task of filtering through a wide range of issues: complex non-linear histories, globalization, a new cosmopolitanism, extremes in wealth and poverty, political and religious conservatism, environmental degradation and an unknown future. There is not as yet a fully articulated sense of Indian design and one must wonder whether, in the end, it will be only high-end luxury design for an incredibly tiny portion of the population that will be celebrated. Or will *jugaad* (makeshift innovation), a sustainable design that involves recycling goods to make new machines or tools and adapting traditional knowledge to create local solutions, become quintessentially 'Indian'? Will there, instead, be cohesion between luxury, sustainability and recycling?

The plethora of natural resources and raw materials that exist within India's geographical spread has been, and still is, instrumental in developing a diversity of objects. During India's historical past, a vast number of foreigners arrived by sea and land in search of her greatest natural resources: spices, cottons, silks, precious metals and stones, teak, ivory, natural dyes, to name only a few. The abundance of indigenous materials has provided designers and artisans with endless ways in which to explore nature and materiality through form and function, and also allowed them to make important choices between using sustainable and unsustainable materials.

Design schools have mushroomed around the country and budding designers are also going abroad to study, returning to India with new perspectives. At the same time, contemporary designers working beyond national borders or travelling back and forth to India, as part of the larger diaspora, integrate elements of 'Indian-ness' in their work, like London-based studio Doshi Levien. Contemporary designers today bear the responsibility of understanding what crafts exist in India and how to work with them. For example, designers such as Sandeep Sangaru (b. 1975) are dedicated to working in bamboo, through initiation by Professor M.P. Ranjan (1950–2015) at the National Institute of Design, whose work, research and efforts at finding an indigenous language and material for design was passionate and relentless. In addition, it is essential that today's designers understand how to support the *karigars* (skilled artisans), such as weavers, metalsmiths and *kumhars* (potters). These are responsibilities that, if met, could revitalize a national language of Indian design, even perhaps unifying the principles underlying Gandhi's identification with the craftsman, Nehru's desire for good design and Tagore's educational ideals.

Recently, beyond the borders of India, within the greater design community, there has been a renewed interest in India. Non-Indians, like their forefathers before them, come to India in search of her finest resources and develop design practices, both within and outside the country, using Indian techniques, philosophies and crafts to inform their own work. Australian designer Sian Pascale's Bhel Puri side table (page 274) is a formalized interpretation of a commonly seen street object used in selling street food. Luxury European fashion brands, such as Dries van Noten, Balmain and Hermès, have worked in India for decades to create high-end embroideries. As India evolves on the contemporary global stage and the diaspora continues to spread, it is only a matter of time before certain objects become assimilated into global everyday life and negative assumptions related to 'Made in India' will become positive. We can also now alter the prevailing ethnographic view to look at objects not purely in terms of their connection to ritual or their decoration. In recent years there has been a collective change in the more formal presentation of Indian design: international exhibitions include *Living Objects — Made for India* at the Grand-Hornu, Boussu, Belgium, in 2013; *India Past ⋉ Forward* at Millesgården, Lidingö, near Stockholm, in 2015; and *Fabric of India* at the Victoria and Albert Museum, London, in 2015. These events contemplate and showcase how the past can inform the future, while offering viewers a detailed insight into contemporary Indian life. This new and evolving landscape would welcome a permanent museum dedicated to Indian historical and contemporary design.

The 5,000-year-old past is not superior, nor idyllic, nor pure, but it undeniably belongs to the future of a young nation that is in the process of defining and articulating its identity. Designers in this vast, complicated, fast-moving country have a number of issues to work out. If design is truly to come into its own, there needs to be a convergence between beauty and aesthetics, utility, sustainability and improved manufacturing. Innovative designs need to be made in answer to that 'deeper hunger of humanity', for the masses, to be accessible and to be widely applicable. If the social and economic status of the craftsman can be made equal to that of a 'designer', the potential for creative and financial growth is immense. Designing for the twenty-first century should become a formally studied concept and applied to all aspects of life — integrated into policy making and business strategy and embraced by ordinary people as a means of improving the *sār* of life. Design is a field that belongs to all periods and all cultures. *Sār: The Essence of Indian Design* has given us the opportunity to survey the past through contemporary language and terminology. Shaping, forming, problem-solving, building, constructing, moulding, storing, wearing, eating — all these have always existed, but maybe 'design' could be made the new construct that binds together all these shared and connected activities, or perhaps there could be the invention of a new word altogether.

1   An ancient civilization located by the Indus River running between Pakistan and northwest India, from around 5500 to 1900 BC.

2   The period before the economic reforms of 1991 implemented by Dr Manmohan Singh, Minister of Finance from 1991–6, which permitted foreign companies to enter the Indian market.

3   Divya Thakur, *India Past ⋉ Forward* (Millesgården, Stockholm, 2015), 4.

4   Alvin C. Moore, Jr., foreword to Ananda K. Coomaraswamy, *The Indian Craftsman* (Munshiram Manoharlal Publishers, New Delhi, 1909), 1.

5   Jasleen Dhamija, *Indian Folk Arts and Crafts* (National Book Trust, New Delhi, 1970), 2.

6   Vidya Deheja, *Indian Art* (Phaidon Press, London, 1997), 13.

7   Saloni Mathur, *India by Design: Colonial History and Cultural Display* (University of California Press, Hyderabad, 2007), 10.

8   Rabindranath Tagore, *Nationalism* (Penguin Books, London, 2010).

9   K.G. Subramanyan, *Do Hands Have a Chance?* (Seagull Books, Calcutta, 2007), 5.

10 A craft cluster is an area within a village where the making of crafts takes place, although sometimes the entire village is involved.

11 Charles and Ray Eames, *The India Report* (National Institute of Design, Ahmedabad, 1997).

12 Jyotindra Jain, *Utensils: An Introduction to the Utensils Museum Ahmedabad* (Vechaar, Ahmedabad, 1984), 3.

13 Kamaladevi Chattopadhyay, *Handicrafts of India* (Indian Council for Cultural Relations, New Delhi, 1975), 3.

14 Eames, *The India Report* (Ahmedabad, 1997).

15 Jyotindra Jain, 'Material and Transition Writings' in *India Past ⋉ Forward*, ed. Divya Thakur (Millesgården, Stockholm, 2015).

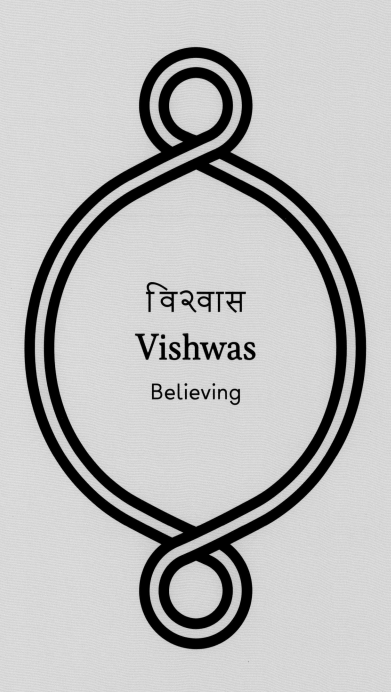

विश्वास

Vishwas

Believing

Kanga

Date 2015
Designer Unknown
Materials Wood

The *kanga*, a simple wooden comb, small enough to tuck neatly into one's hair, is one of the five objects — specifically, articles of faith — that all Sikhs should have in their daily lives. Guru Gobind Singh (1666–1708), the tenth guru of Sikhism, introduced these objects and declared that Sikhs should allow their hair to grow naturally and never be cut, so as to identify them as Sikhs. The *kanga* is used to comb one's hair and keep it clean, while the act of combing one's hair is a reminder to keep life healthy and organized. Wood is preferred to metal or plastic, as it doesn't create any static. It is also softer and less damaging to the scalp and some medicinal woods, such as neem, are used.

Dhupdan

Date 2015
Designer Unknown
Materials Brass

Burning *dhoop* — which is incense in stick or cone form — releases a very intense scent and smoke and is popularly made of *chandan* (sandalwood), which is primarily farmed in Kerala and Karnataka. The *dhoop* is placed in the upper cup of the brass *dhupdan*, a traditional vessel, which is shaped like a *damru* (drum), representing the hourglass-shaped instrument from which Lord Shiva sounds the beginning of Creation. The handle of this *dhupdan* has curves for the thumb and index finger so that one can easily hold and rotate it in a clockwise direction while the incense is burning, as part of a Hindu prayer or *puja*, to offer respect to a deity or to ward off demons.

←

Toran

Date 2015
Designer Unknown
Materials Cotton, silk thread, mirror

In Hinduism, the entrance to a space should signify that something meaningful and special lies beyond and the *toran* (meaning archway or gate), which is hung in front of doorways, symbolizes this concept. In their most natural form, *torans* consist of sacred mango or ashoka (*Saraca asoca*) leaves strung on cotton threads. In arid regions where trees are scarce, such as western Gujarat and Rajasthan, brightly appliquéd fabrics, embroidery and tassels are used to replicate the leaves instead. Small mirrors attached to the *toran* are believed to ward off evil spirits by blinding them with their own reflections, as well as providing light and energy. A means of protection, they are strung at the top of front doors, particularly during religious and wedding ceremonies. The use of *torans* is detailed in the *Vastu Shastra*, which are ancient Indian texts on the science of architecture.

Chowki

Date Early twentieth century
Designer Unknown
Materials Lacquered wood

Before European-style furniture was introduced during colonialism, Indian furniture consisted of pieces like this low *chowki*, which is raised up on four legs. It can be made from oxidized silver with *meenakari* work, brass, plain wood or, like this example, lacquered wood. The *chowki* is used for seating or is situated in an area in the home or office that is intended for prayer, when idols are placed on top of it. A *chowki* is typically square with one level but this example, from Gujarat, has an octagonal secondary level, and is generally larger than most. Northern Kutch, Gujarat has a tradition of wood carving and turning, creating geometric patterns with shallow relief, which can be seen in this design.

Papier mâché masks

Date 2010
Designer Dhanalakota Nageshwar
Materials Mud, sawdust, cow dung, paper

Mask-maker Dhanalakota Nageshwar created these papier mâché masks in 2010 as an exploration of the long tradition of mask-making in India, where masks are used in storytelling or as a means of warding off evil spirits. Nageshwar's masks do not have a ritual purpose, but are objects of contemplation on the medium of papier mâché. The process of papier mâché is practised by many artisans in India who work with a basic mould comprised of mud, sawdust and cow dung, which is then covered in paper or sometimes cotton rags. The image of the face is painted using watercolours made from vegetable dyes. Common motifs are animals in folklore that are related to Hindu texts and mythology and also those of everyday life such as the cow, horse, tiger and elephant.

←

Bindi stickers

Date 2015
Designer Bhumika Bindi
Materials Flock velvet fabric, adhesive

Look at a mirror in an Indian household and you are likely to notice one or more bindis stuck on the side to be reused. The bindi is a traditional, red, circular marking placed between the eyebrows, which symbolizes the sixth chakra (the third eye) and the marking of a married woman. Bindi stickers emerged during the 1960s as a quick and easy way to place a red mark on the forehead perfectly. The back is covered in adhesive while the front has a velvet-like texture created by flocking. Prior to the stickers, there was the *tilak* bindi which required a laborious process of taking a little disc, applying wax, then applying *sindoor* powder (zinc oxide and dye) or *kumkum* (red turmeric powder). Once the little disc was dipped in the bright-red powder, it was skilfully applied directly to the area between the eyebrows with the tip of the ring finger and the disc was then carefully removed leaving behind a perfect circle. Today, sticker bindis can be found with little jewels, in highly decorative forms or multicoloured, but it is the red or maroon bindi that is most common, as red signifies love and prosperity.

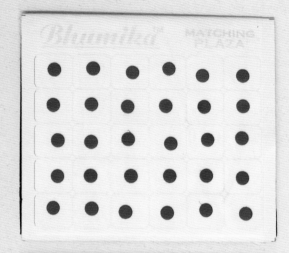

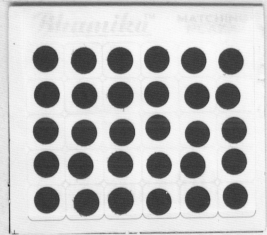

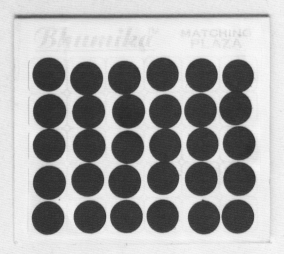

Ogho or Rajoharan

Date 2014
Designer Unknown
Materials Wool, wood

Jainism emerged in India at about the same time as Buddhism — around the sixth century BC — as a way to escape the Hindu caste system. Jains believe that a monastic life of self-denial can liberate the soul and that one can achieve nirvana in this life. They also believe that all things — plants, insects, animals — have souls of equal value so they are strict vegetarians and consume in a way that has the least affect on natural resources. The Svetambara sect of Jains cover their mouths with a *Muhapatti*, or piece of white cloth, to avoid swallowing insects and carry the *Ogho* or *Rajoharan* to sweep the ground as they walk or before they sit, to avoid killing any living thing. The brooms are traditionally composed of woollen strands with a short handle and the monks and nuns are often seen carrying them, as a symbol of their monastic vows. When initiated into Jainism, by denouncing the material world, the initiate is given the *Ogho* or *Rajoharan* by a mentor during a ritual.

Copper yantra

Date 2015
Designer Unknown
Materials Copper

When this thin copper plate is placed in the home, on the ground or even on a stone, the area around it is deemed ready for meditation. *Yantras* are instruments or tools used in spiritual pursuits and are made either in two-dimensional form, known as *Bhu*, or in pyramid form, known as *Meru*. There are many types of *yantra* — some devoted to a specific god or goddess, some for wealth, some for overcoming evil and some for bringing good luck into the home. *Yantras* have been used historically within esoteric practices of major religions like Hinduism, Buddhism and Jainism.

←

Parsi sace

Date 2014
Designer Unknown
Materials Nickel silver, stainless steel

The *sace* is a ceremonial tray used by Parsis, the Zoroastrian community in India, for marriage ceremonies, *navjote* (initiation) and for *Nowruz* — the New Year. The tray is filled with various items depending on the occasion. The modern example seen here is a mini tray with symbolic objects: the *soparo* (a cone representing a mountain of sweetness that in older times, would have been made out of a kind of rock-sugar), the *gulabaz* (rose-water sprinkler) and the *pigani* (a container that holds *kumkum*, or red powder). The tray, which must have a high rim, will also be covered with rose petals, a garland of flowers, pistachios, coins, betel nut and *paan* leaves, along with a coconut, an egg, rice grains, dried dates, sugar crystals and *patasa* (a traditional candy), wood and frankincense, all of which signify various virtues and blessings. In most cases, the *sace* is passed down through generations as a family heirloom. The Zoroastrian religion dates back approximately 3,500 years and Parsis came to India from Iran between the eight and tenth centuries AD.

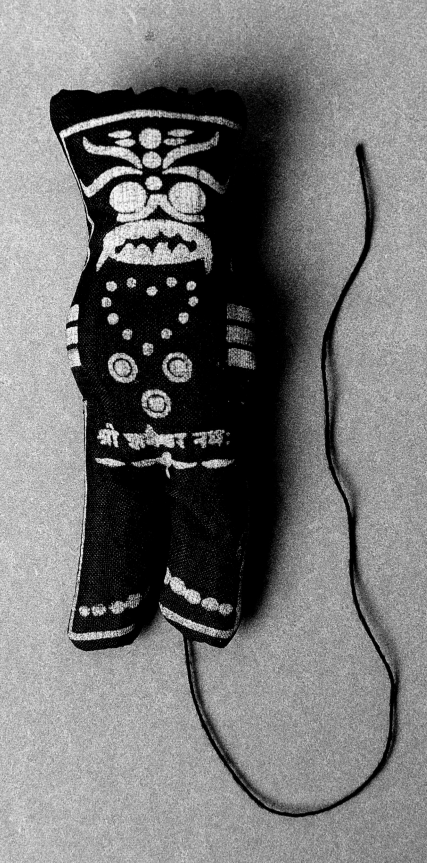

Bell Luce

Date 2011
Designer IndiaUrban
Materials Powder-coated aluminium, electroplated brass

IndiaUrban's Bell Luce lights evoke the spirit and sounds of temple bells, which are a fundamental part of prayers in India. When entering a Hindu temple it is customary to ring the bells, much like an announcement, but also in order to experience and connect with their vibrations. The metal temple bells perfectly transmit sounds and vibrations and the Bell Luce transmits light — another source of energy. Made of electroplated brass and powder-coated aluminium, the hanging light looks to India's metal-making past while moving Indian design forward.

Bahuli

Date 2014
Designer Unknown
Materials Cotton, paint

The importance of protecting oneself and one's home is evident in the number of items known collectively as *nazar battu*, which are intended to ward off an evil eye or bad intentions. While protection from *nazar* (evil eye) is a centuries-old tradition found throughout India, it is also found in Arab countries and Pakistan. The protection can take different forms: one way is to introduce a flaw to an item, such as a small error in a pattern; another is to hang a *totka* (a string of seven chillies and one lime) or *bahuli* (doll in Marathi) from an entrance, car, rickshaw or back of a lorry. The doll ranges from 6 cm to at least 17 cm (2⅓ in to 6⅔ in) in height and is typically made from black cotton, stuffed with cotton and decorated with white paint. Some also have colourful painted faces. The design incorporates a thread so that the *bahuli* can hang upside down from a doorway beam or the rear-view mirror of a car.

←

Janamaz or Sajada

Date 2011
Designer Unknown
Materials Nylon, cotton

Essential to daily Islamic prayers is the *janamaz*, an individual prayer rug on which a devotee prostrates himself towards Mecca. Tracing the visual history of the rugs reveals many design variations and colours. This modern example features a bold and graphic depiction of the Kaaba, the building at the centre of the Great Mosque in Mecca. Generally the small 60 x 120-cm (26 x 48-in) rugs have a depiction of the *mihrab* — the shallow architectural niche found in the *qiblah*, the holy Mecca-facing wall in a mosque — woven into them. Once the correct location of Mecca is determined, the *mihrab* on the rug is pointed in that direction, much like a compass, and the devotee kneels down and places his forehead on the *janamaz*, facing towards the Kaaba. Before inexpensive machine-woven carpets made of synthetic blends were mass-produced, handwoven carpets were used and they often still are.

Sindoor box

Date 2015
Designer Unknown
Materials Mango wood, lacquer

The simple, evocative shape and rich, glossy red colour make this hand-lathed wooden *sindoor* box from Dumraon in Bihar graphic and striking. Like many small objects, its form is based on Hindu temples and spires, believed to transmit cosmic energies into physical spaces and objects. *Sindoor*, which is a reddish-orange vermilion powder, is applied by Hindu women to the middle parting on their foreheads to signify that they are married and a fertile life force. The first time *sindoor* is applied is by a woman's husband at their wedding ceremony and from then on it is applied daily until widowhood. A *sindoor dibbi* is a smaller, transportable version that a woman will make or buy herself, use for daily application and refill when empty. Made throughout India to this day, *sindoor* boxes come in a variety of shapes and sizes and can be plain red or feature carvings, inlays and appliqués. Marble and silver are also used in the making of these small containers.

←

Lingam candle

Date 2012
Designer IndiaUrban
Materials Wax

India's religious traditions provide a starting point for some contemporary designers, and sculptural representations of the god Shiva and the lingam were the inspiration for this candle — a phallus form perfectly housed in the female *yoni*-shaped basin — that symbolizes the dualities of female and male energies and the cosmic life force. Solid, smooth and shiny, the satisfying form of the candle, which evokes brilliant white marble, is made of a dripless wax and comes in white or black. The phallus burns first, followed by the round *yoni* base, and creates a brilliant glow, as a metaphor for our inner spiritual fire.

Puja ghar

Date 2015
Designer Unknown
Materials Acrylic

Hindu religious images and devotional objects can be seen throughout the landscape of India. A mini *puja ghar* (prayer house) is useful in small spaces and is often seen in places of business, close to the cash area. Images of deities or small idols and other ephemera, such as flowers and *diyas* (page 62), are placed here to pray for success and prosperity. The basic structure of the *puja ghar* is traditionally based on the principles of Hindu temple architecture, and features a pyramid-like top called the *shikhara* (holy mountain top) that houses the deity or ephemera below. A small drawer in front is used to store ritual items like matches, cotton, incense and threads. They can be made of marble, wood or silver. This modern example is made of acrylic, an affordable and lightweight option that is easy to mount on the wall. The saffron colour represents *agni* (fire), symbolic of the supreme being.

Ghantis

Date Early twentieth century
Designer Unknown
Materials Brass

Cosmic and spiritual energy are transmitted through the sounds and vibrations of *ghantis* (Hindu temple bells). The elegant forms of the brass bells are rung by devotees and priests to announce their arrival to the gods while evoking the sounds of Om. Hand-cast by metalsmiths across the country, bell metal or bronze is traditionally used in making a variety of *ghantas* (larger bells) and *ghantis* (smaller bells). The hard metal, combined with a proportionate weight and shape, is ideal for transmitting the correct pitch and providing a depth of sound. Two types of bell are found suspended in temples or in private home temples — one is a *ghungroo* style, which is a hollow sphere with a loose metal ball inside, and the other style, which is more common at temples, is cup-shaped with a clapper to be rung by devotees. Animals, such as birds, cows and peacocks, and mythological figures that relate to a specific god may adorn the top of the bell. Handheld *ghantis* are also used during prayers.

←

Gulabdani

Date Early twentieth century
Designer Unknown
Materials White brass

Greeting your guests with a sprinkle of rose water is a custom inherited from the Persians of the Mughal period. Rose water appears in food, in perfume and has long been used for its inherent cooling and nutritional qualities. The *gulabdani* has a long neck topped with a floral-shaped head that has small perforations. It is opened at the base of the neck and the body filled with rose water, which is then held in one's hand and shaken to release the fragrant water. The *gulabdani* has entered Hindu customs and is used during rituals, for sprinkling rose water over guests or over a new bride. Bhuj in Gujarat is well known for *gulabdani*s produced in brass and metal with detailed engraving, filigree or relief work, as is Nasik in Maharashtra for its work in sheet metal.

Ayigalu or Shivadhara

Date Early twentieth century
Designer Lingayat sect
Materials Silver

The Lingayats, a sect that emerged in the state of Karnataka in the twelfth century, rejected Brahman authority, encouraged equality between men and women, allowed the remarriage of widows and worshipped an iconic representation of Shiva as a pillar (*stambha*). Not believing in the construction of temples led to a transportable, nomadic practice of worship, using the *jangama lingam* — a small, movable stone that is stored upright and an abstract representation of the god Shiva. The design of the Ayigalu was created as a way to perpetually carry his form everywhere. It is made in sandalwood, copper, silver or gold, and its shape is a metaphor for the golden egg, or the Creator. It is held between two pillars topped by pyramid-like shapes decorated with circular finials through which a cord is passed to make a necklace. Thus the Ayigalu can be carried on the body at all times and easily opened in order to unwrap the red or white cotton square that contains the soapstone lingam (which is further protected by a layer of lac, clay and cow dung ashes). This vessel is an example of how design followed function.

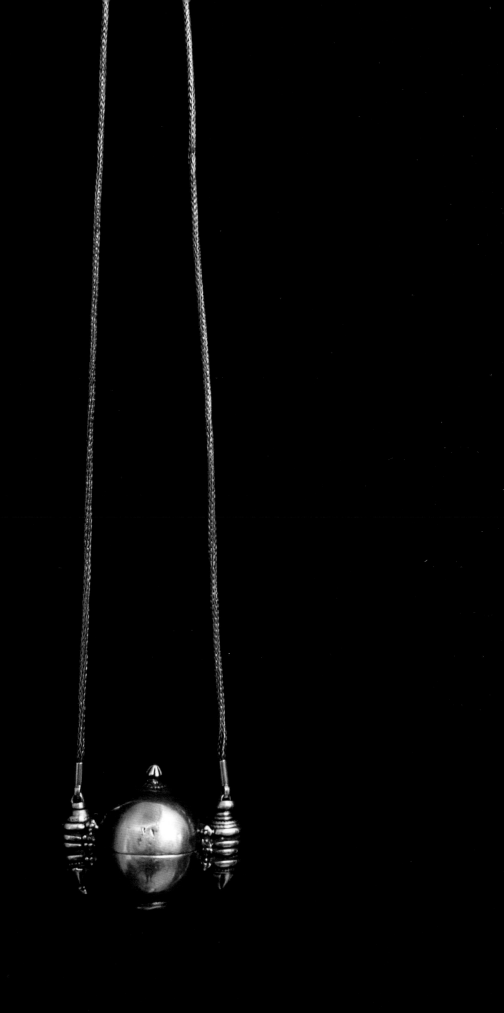

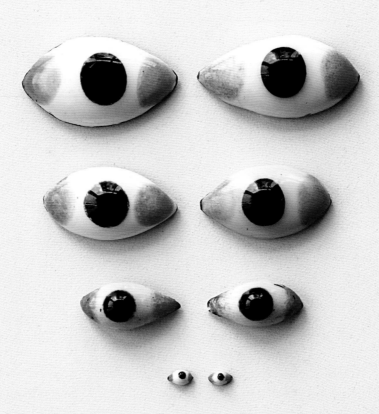

Modak mould

Date 2015
Designer Unknown
Materials Aluminium

Ukadiche modak are steamed, rice-flour dumplings filled with a mixture of jaggery (unrefined sugar), grated coconut, cardamom and poppy seeds and are made in moulds with painstaking care. The interior of the mould is first coated with ghee, then it is closed and rice-flour dough pressed along the inner walls. The interior cavity is then filled with the jaggery mixture and sealed with more rice dough. The mould is unhinged to reveal a perfect teardrop shaped *modak*, which is steamed for around ten minutes. *Modak* originated in the state of Maharashtra and are believed to be the favourite dish of the elephant-headed god, Ganesha. They are commonly made in late August or September for the two-week-long Ganesha festival when twenty-one *modaks* are offered to Lord Ganesha. *Modak* moulds have two hinges and come in a variety of materials, including stainless steel, plastic and aluminium (as seen in this example from 2015).

←

Ceramic god eyes

Date 2015
Designer Unknown
Materials Clay, paint

Open eyes are channels for light and energy and connect us to one another. Eyes on *murthis* (idols), Hindu anthropomorphic deities that are manifestations of the divine spirit, are generally depicted as open in order to connect the worshipper to the holy. Statues of Hindu gods and goddesses range from the minute to the magnificent and are found in temples or paraded through the streets during festivals. The guidelines for the size, proportions and expression of the eyes on them are detailed in the *Shilpa Shastras*, ancient Sanskrit texts on the science of the arts and crafts. Inexpensive, industrially manufactured ceramic eyes are available in various sizes and are sold separately because some statues are produced without eyes and taken to places of worship where eyes are then affixed to symbolize the deity coming to life.

Bomma

Date 2010
Designer S. Anjaneyulu
Materials Dyed animal hide, bamboo

Nowadays symbols of an age-old tradition struggling to survive in today's culture of mass media and entertainment, *bomma* (shadow puppets) are delightful examples of traditional storytelling — tales from the two epic works of Indian literature, the *Ramayana* and *Mahabharata*, being the most popular. They stand 90 cm to 180 cm (35 in to 70 in) tall and are made from two to three reinforced deer, goat or buffalo hides. The hand-cut skins, which are semi-translucent, are hand-painted with vegetable dyes on both sides. Handstitched joints for legs and arms and a series of bamboo splints attached to the back allow the puppet-eer to manipulate the *bomma*, delighting audiences with their narratives. The puppeteers perform behind a white sheet that is illuminated with ample light so that the colours and shapes of the *bomma* shine through. The artist S. Anjane-yulu (b. 1959), who created this *bomma*, hails from a long-standing family of puppet makers and is dedicated to keeping the performing puppets alive, rather than simply offer-ing them as souvenir or 'craft' objects for sale.

Bhiksha patra

Date 2015
Designer Ayush Kasliwal, Anantaya Decor
Materials Rohida wood

Bhiksha patra are alms vessels used by the monks of the Jain Svetambara sect. These elegant bowls are hand-lathed by Kharadis — Muslim craftsmen in Rajasthan who trace their ancestral practice to Mughal times. The finely-walled nesting bowls, available in sets of three to sixteen, are each made out of one section of rohida wood — a native tree (*Tecomella undulata*) found in the Thar Desert. No part of the wood is left wasted, the smaller bowl being skilfully carved out of the heart of the larger bowl and the walls of each bowl are approximately 1.5 mm thick. The white-robed Svetambara monks, who renounce all worldly possessions and journey on foot, are given the *bhiksha patra* as *daana* (religious gifts) to use to receive offerings and to carry and store food. They are seen as an extension of their non-materialist way of life. Monks may paint their bowls with lacquer in colours of red, white and black to strengthen the wood and as a means of identification. When the bowls are no longer in use they are broken into pieces, buried and return to earth. The examples seen here were designed and made for Anantaya Decor.

←

Kamandal

Date 1990s
Designer Unknown
Materials Brass

Wandering ascetics (sadhus) are those who have renounced all worldly possessions in search of *moksha* — release from the cycle of rebirth. They do carry and keep a few necessary belongings though, such as the clothes on their backs and the *kamandal* — a vessel used to carry holy water and food or to collect offerings that can be found in early Hindu iconography. It may also be used in ritual practices. The relevance of nature in design aesthetics is applied to many objects and vessels for cooking, eating and drinking, including the *kamandal*, for which gourds and coconuts act as the design prototype. Brass, gourds, clay, coconut and wood are some of the materials used to make *kamandals* — the example here is a hand-cast brass version with a narrow opening for the intention of carrying holy water. Many sadhus prefer natural gourds, however, as they are lightweight, do not react with the food and give a greater sense of impermanence.

Kavad

Date 2015
Designer Kumawat caste
Materials Neem wood, poster paint, varnish

Part of India's oral storytelling traditions, the *kavad* is a three-dimensional, portable wooden shrine that contains multiple hinged panels, each hand-painted and decorated with various themes from Hindu mythology, as in this example from 2015. The *kavariyas* (religious storytellers) commission families of artisans belonging to the Kumawat caste from Bassi in southern Rajasthan, to create these delightful mobile shrines. The design of the *kavad* is engineered to flow with the story — as it unfolds, so do the doors, which are opened one after the other. Generally, three-dimensional deities are placed in the innermost chamber and are revealed at the end of the story. *Kavads* range in size; some are small enough to fit in one's hands while others are as large as a wardrobe. Little drawers and compartments are also built into the sides for storage of frequently required items, such as incense or a pointer stick, and for collecting donations.

Rudraksha mala

Date 2009
Designer Unknown
Materials Seeds, cotton thread

Rudraksha malas, associated with wandering ascetics or sadhus, are believed to have healing, protective and divine powers. Wearing a traditional *mala* (necklace) of 108 beads is believed to increase confidence, give one a sense of peacefulness and is recommended for various bodily ailments. The *rudraksha* bead is a seed that comes from a fruit with a blueberry-like exterior and grows on a tree (*Elaeocarpus ganitrus*) found primarily in the northern regions of India. Each seed has a certain number of faces (*mukhis*) and a hole in the centre. They are strung on either cotton or silk to be used as a rosary by Hindus and Buddhists for *japa* (mantras). It is believed that pressing each seed between the thumb and middle finger, as the *mala* is held, is a form of acupressure that benefits circulation in particular parts of the body. In Sanskrit lore, *rudraksha* comes from the tears of the Lord Shiva, *rudra* meaning 'Shiva' and *aksha* meaning 'tears'. It is believed that as Lord Shiva woke from deep meditation, great tears fell from his eyes and became the roots of the *rudraksha* tree.

←

Iyengar yoga blocks

Date 2015
Designer B.K.S. Iyengar Institute
Materials Pinewood

The use of props while practising yoga asanas (positions) was introduced by B.K.S. Iyengar (1918–2014), who began teaching yoga in Pune at the age of eighteen. Iyengar believed that providing support during an asana — using blankets, wall ropes, sandbags, chairs or benches — could help one relax into the posture and deepen one's alignment, regardless of age, injuries or general physical condition. His variety of yoga focuses on building weaker muscles instead of relying on already developed muscles to hold positions. The use of props helps a student gain a better understanding of how to hold a position and build their confidence. Iyengar suggested that the blocks be hollow, made with a light wood such as pine, balsa or bamboo, and that the dimensions be 23 x 12 x 7 cm (9 x 4¾ x 2¾ in), with each block weighing no more than 1.13 kg (2½ lb). These simple blocks are used to support the hands, the head, the hips and the knees. The blocks pictured here — in pine and with rounded edges — were made to order via the B.K.S. Iyengar Institute in Mumbai.

←

Patang

Date 2015
Designer Unknown
Materials Paper, bamboo, cotton

Uttarayan is a kite festival that is held every 14 January throughout Gujarat to celebrate the arrival of summer and the harvest season. From 5 a.m. onwards the sky is seen dotted with brightly coloured *patang*, or kites, each made from a fine piece of paper shaped into a rhombus, with a central bamboo spine attached to a slightly bowed, horizontal splint. The splints are held securely with tiny pieces of paper that have been glued down by a kitemaker. He sits cross-legged at a low wooden table, where he rhythmically folds and glues in one rapid motion. A string is sewn through the paper and is used by the flyer to manoeuvre the kite. This string is a cotton thread that has been coated with starch and glass powder to create a sharp line, called a *manja*. Although the kites are incredibly thin and appear flimsy, with great skill and devotion the kite flyers are able to duel, the aim being to cut through the string of one's opponent. The *patang* bazaar, where the kites are made, stays open the whole twenty-four hours during the festival, fulfilling the great demand of people of all ages, backgrounds and religions. Demand is so high that craftsmen travel to Gujarat from as far as Uttar Pradesh and Bihar.

Taweez or Ta'wiz

Date 2008
Designer Unknown
Materials Silver, wax, velvet

Traditional amulets or talismans used for protection are called *taweez* by Muslims in India. The minimalist design of the *taweez* contains sacred verses, mystical text and numbers to protect the wearer from evil and ensure good health. These are written on pieces of paper and each is placed in a silver or aluminium pendant in the shape of a thin box or cylinder. The small pendants are covered in wax for protection, then encased in handstitched velvet pouches and strung on a black thread to be worn around the neck. The *taweez* should be worn at all times and when the fabric casing becomes old or dirty it is replaced with a new one. Black is used in a lot of objects, as it is believed by many religions and sects in India to ward off evil eyes.

←

Nazar battu

Date 2015
Designer Unknown
Materials Clay, paint

Staring down from above doorways of homes or shops are horrific faces with large, lined, googly eyes and dark-red tongues. Handmade in papier mâché or clay and hand-painted, these traditional masks are slightly smaller than an adult face. Called *nazar battu*, their purpose is to draw the evil eye towards them in order to defeat it, and the uglier or scarier they are, the better. The saying 'buri nazar waale tera muh kala' (you who regard us with an evil eye, may your face be blackened) is the superstitious belief behind the protection of the mask, which is used by Muslims, Hindus and Jains. There are many design variations — some are painted in white, red or yellow.

←

Niranjan or Vilakku

Date Mid-nineteenth century
Designer Pathar community
Materials Brass

The city of Thanjavur was the seat of the Chola Kingdom during the ninth century AD and famous for the tradition of bronze and brass casting, used in the production of musical instruments, idols, repoussé plates and lamps. This lamp was made by the Pathar community — originally from the very south of India and traditionally gold- and silversmiths, they moved towards Thanjavur in the nineteenth century because of the light-brown sand along the banks of the River Kaveri, which they used for mould casts for this type of lamp and for temple bells. The lamp, or *vilakku*, is first formed from mud or wood, which is then cast in brass. The base, stem and top plate for holding the wicks are each made separately using a box mould. The ornamented head of the lamp would have been made using *cire perdue*, or the lost-wax method. These lamps, with tiny grooves for holding the wicks, are lit each day as dusk arrives, or used for worship in temples. They range in size from 10 cm to anything up to 3 m (4 in to 10 ft).

Bohra topi

Date 2015
Designer Unknown
Materials Cotton, gold thread

Bohra topis, almost cake-like in their appearance, are delicately hand-crocheted by women using cotton thread and *kasab* (gold thread) and are worn by Muslim men of the Dawoodi Bohra community in Gujarat. With the exception of an occasional thin black or green border, white and gold (as shown in this example from 2015) are the most common colours to be used on the caps and more gold is added for special occasions. Plastic and aluminium blocks are used to keep the caps' shape while crocheting. *Bohra topis* are usually worn with a crisp white *kurta* pyjama and white jacket.

←

Diyas

Date 2015
Designer Unknown
Materials Clay

Lighting the exterior of a home is a welcoming sign, not only for guests or to mark festivals such as Diwali (the start of the Hindu New Year and 'festival of lights'), but also to welcome Lakshmi, the goddess of wealth. As dusk arrives, *diyas* are placed on the ground outside the entrances to homes. A *diya* is a small earthenware votive, filled with *ghee* (clarified butter) or vegetable oil. A hand-rolled cotton wick rests on the small indentation, partially submerged in the oil. Clay votives date back to the Indus Valley Civilization, when earthen-ware and terracotta potters' wheels were first used. The examples seen here are simple handmade *diyas* but they are also available in all kinds of machine-moulded shapes and can be ornately decorated.

←

Lung ta

Date 2010
Designer Unknown
Materials Nylon

Tibetan prayer flags are short and hung horizontally (*Lung ta*) or vertically (*Darchor*). In the Himalayas, from the tops of temples and monasteries, these traditional flags are strung up so that the hollowing wind of the mountains carries their messages across wide valleys. They are always hung in the order of blue, white, red, green and yellow, representing the five elements. The flags are block-printed with the central motif of the *Lung ta* — the Wind Horse, which is believed to carry the energy of the body that the mind relies on. The mantras printed around the image are dedicated to deities connected with Bon — a shamanistic religion originating in Tibet and closely related to Tibetan Buddhism. Block-printing on flags began during the arrival of Buddhism in Tibet, with an Indian monk who brought the practice of printing on cloth banners. The flags carry ephemeral prayers for peoples in exile. In 1959, many Tibetans, along with their religious leader H.H. the Dalai Lama, fled to India due to Chinese occupation. As a result, most of the Tibetan diaspora has large communities in Bhutan and Nepal, and about 1,000,000 Tibetans in India.

सजना-सवरना

Sajna Savarna

Decorating

Uruli, Vattalam, Vaarpu

Date Early twenty-first century
Designer Moosari community
Materials Brass

Beautifully proportioned, with a wide circular opening and a shallow convex base, the distinctive *uruli* was originally a cooking vessel from Kerala. Its wide surface area ensured good heat distribution from the fire and created perfectly cooked dishes. A distinctive feature of *urulis* are the outward-curved metal loops, stylized as creepers, to slide rods through for carrying the vessel if it is especially heavy. Metalsmiths of the Moosari community, especially in Shoranur, Kerala, have been creating *urulis* for generations, laboriously casting them in bell metal or brass using the *cire perdue,* or lost-wax method, a process that can take several days. Cooking with *urulis* has declined in past decades as they are expensive and very heavy, but they have become popular decorative objects, used for floating flowers in water instead.

Classical Lotus Chhatra Light

Date 2014
Designer Valay Gada, Cobalt Designs
Materials Brass

The *chhatra* is a parasol that appears in Hindu and Buddhist imagery and iconography as a symbol of both protection and royalty. Often a *chhatra* is seen hanging over an icon or appears, made from textiles, on mammoth floats that, for the purposes of public display and celebration, carry images of gods and goddesses outside of temples. Valay Gada (b. 1980), Delhi-based artist, designer and founder of Cobalt Designs, has taken this familiar emblem and adapted it to create a hanging lamp. Gada was paying his respects at a Jain temple when, looking at the *chhatra* images, he realized that the design could become a light source. He collaborated with metalsmiths in Old Delhi and Moradabad, who used the repoussé technique on a sheet of brass after it was hammered into a bowl-like shape to produce these lotus flower motifs. The piece was then acid washed to create a yellow, matt finish. Although the shape is still rooted in traditional language, Gada achieves a contemporary result through the use of craft techniques.

←

Wooden printing block

Date 2015
Designer Unknown
Materials Sal wood

India's textile history is so rich and many objects and tools, such as this block, are an integral part of its creation process. Master craftsmen handcarve these beautiful wooden blocks, which are used for block printing on cloth. Preferred woods are teak, shisham or sal, as they are strong and do not warp with the use of water and paints. Blocks are made for single or multiple patterns and endless designs, including geometrics, florals, trellises and quatrefoils, can be etched onto them. Once the size, which can range from 2.5 to 40.5 cm (1 to 16 in), and the shape of the block are determined, the surface is painted white and the motif drawn on. The craftsman then carves out the design using chisels and manually operated hand drills and bows. To allow for the passage of air when printing, holes are drilled into the back of the block and registration marks are notched in to ensure seamless pattern alignment.

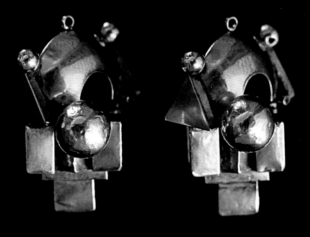

Kajrota or Surmadani

Date 2015
Designer Unknown
Materials Brass and cast iron

Kohl, called *kajal* or *surma*, is stibnite, a mineral that turns black with oxidization and has been used for centuries to line the eyes. For young children, in particular, kohl is believed to provide protection from *nazar*, or the evil eye. It is either applied to the eyes of the child, or on a point on their body to create a flaw. Women across the Middle East use kohl, lining from the inner to the outer rim of the eye using a stick, and in India, men in certain regions will line their eyes with it, some as a daily ritual or on festive occasions. Kohl is also used for Ayurvedic treatment of the eyes, believed to strengthen them and provide protection from sun damage. Making it with a *kajrota* is simple: a cotton wick is dipped in ghee, lit and placed in the bowl of the *kajrota* until soot collects on the inside of the lid. This soot is then mixed with castor oil and various other ingredients, such as camphor or almond oil. The traditional *kajrota* — shown here in brass and in cast iron — is also used to store the kohl.

←

Thandatti

Date Early twentieth century
Designer Unknown
Materials Lac, gold plated sheet metal

Thandatti earrings are one of many styles that hang off distended earlobes and are worn from the beginning of a girl's life, a time-honoured practice that is found in some parts of the subcontinent but primarily in Tamil Nadu. Possibly influenced by images of Buddha, stretched earlobes are thought to indicate wealth, dignity and wisdom. Here, gold-covered sheet metal is fashioned round a core made of lac. The earlobe sits in between the upper circular section and the cube-like parts, which are hinged and joined by a screw. The geometric form of a *thandatti* is intended to represent a *yantra* (page 30) in a three-dimensional format.

Phulkari

Date Mid-twentieth century
Designer Unknown
Materials Silk floss, cotton cloth

Phulkari (flower work) embroidery from Punjab in fine silk floss is used on *odhnis* (shawls or veils) or *chaddars* (wraps). The technique is believed to have been influenced by Persian *gulkari* embroidery (*gul* meaning 'flower' and *kari* meaning 'work') or by the Jat tribes who migrated to Punjab from Central Asia. According to popular tradition, when a female is born, her grandmother will lovingly begin the process of making her *phulkari* for her future bridal trousseau. The base fabric is a coarse cotton *khaddar* that is locally handspun and handwoven in widths of 1.1 m to 1.5 m (3.7 ft to 5 ft) and joined in panels to the desired size. The cotton is then naturally dyed brown or red, which is considered auspicious. Bright colours, such as reds, pinks, oranges and golds, however, are also common. Geometric floral motifs are then embroidered on the monochrome base fabric. One characteristic of the *phulkari*, which at first glance seems like a mistake, is the introduction of another colour, distorted geometry or an unfinished edge, but this is done purposely to protect the wearer from the evil eye.

Rani ki kangi

Date Mid-twentieth century
Designer Unknown
Materials Shisham

In India, long, dark shiny hair is a sign of beauty, health and femininity. To this end, treatments — such as massaging with oils, scenting with charcoal or dying with henna — are numerous. Hair is adorned with ornaments that are highly elaborate and combs are traditionally made from shell, ivory, bone and wood. Ebony combs are typically made in pairs — male and female: teeth on both sides indicates a female comb (*rani ki kangi*) while the male comb (*raja ki kangi*) has teeth on only one side, but is much more decorative and has a longer handle. These combs are made by small clusters of Muslim craftsmen in Nagina and Bijnor, a town and city in Uttar Pradesh known for wooden craft-making that dates back 300 years. The craftsmen used to use the beautiful, blackish-red ebony wood but today they work with shisham, which is slightly cheaper. Shihsam, or *Dalbergia sissoo*, is a deep brownish-red wood with a texture ideal for carving and native to Nepal, India and Pakistan. A single piece of wood is cut with the teeth carved into one side, without carrying out any measurements beforehand. The decorative engraving is completed using a hand drill.

←

Rohida Shikhar Tiffin

Date 2007
Designer Ayush Kasliwal, Anantaya Decor
Materials Rohida wood, lac

Tiffins comprise of stackable food containers and are a typical Indian way of storing, carrying and protecting food (page 138). With the hot climate comes a plethora of insects that can fall into and contaminate the food (sometimes dying during the process). This was the inspiration behind Ayush Kasliwal's contemporary interpretation of the iconic tiffin design, which upholds the Jain philosophy of non-violence. The tiffin's shape is based on the natural form of the *doodhi* or *lauki* gourd and its colourful top is inspired by a *shikhara* — the spire of a Hindu temple. The rohida wood, which is known for its strength and durability, is hand-lathed by Kharadi craftsmen in Rajasthan. The lacquered spire is made using traditional lac techniques that are typically employed for making lac bangles in the Jaipur area. Lac is a resinous substance produced by the female lac insect found in abundance in Rajasthan's forests.

Mehndi stencils

Date 2015
Designer Unknown
Materials Rubber

Mehndi art uses henna, a paste made out of the henna plant (*Lawsonia inermis*). The leaves of the plant are dried and crushed into a powder, mixed with water and natural herbs and left to soak for a few hours. The result is a thick paste, which, when applied to the skin, leaves a rich reddish-orange stain. Since antiquity, henna's best-known use across the Middle East and Indian subcontinent has been in the creation of intricate decorations on the hands and feet of women. The tradition of decorating the body for festivals and religious holidays is popular in both Hindu and Islamic cultures, particularly during bridal preparations. One or two days before the wedding, a bride and all her female family members gather together and hire a *mehndi* artist. Floral motifs and images of peacocks are drawn on both hands and feet of the bride to symbolize fertility. Although stencils for smaller sections are available, the hand stencils shown here allow for more complex designs. One side is slightly sticky so that it adheres to the hand, following its folds and curves. Unlike other stencils, these modern, rubber versions can be washed and reused.

Panja dhurrie

Date 1990s
Designer Unknown
Materials Cotton

Panja dhurries are woven by women in villages in Punjab and Haryana using geometric and folk patterns that include bird and plant motifs. They are woven from cotton to make a thick fabric that is used for floor coverings in the house or the Sikh Gurdwara, where interiors have sparse furniture. Traditionally, a girl learns to weave early on, as the dhurrie is part of the dowry that she will take to her future husband's home. In order to make a dhurrie, a handloom is set up by securing two poles into the floor and stretching a warp of hand-spun cotton between them, running parallel to the ground and around 15 cm (6 in) above it. Weaving starts at one end, using coloured strands to create the design and the weft, which is pushed in firmly using a *panja* (metal stick). One colour is woven across the full length and interlocked with the next, thereby creating a pattern of multiple threads without any extra weft. The flat weave produces a covering with no backing and no pile, which means that both sides of the dhurrie can be used.

Sandesh moulds

Date 2010
Designer Unknown
Materials Wood

Sandesh (pronounced *shondesh*) is a sweet made from full-fat milk, which is boiled, curdled and strained to make a cottage cheese, which is then cooked with jaggery (unrefined sugar) to yield *makha* — a kind of fudge. While still warm, the *makha* is kneaded and pressed into moulds, such as these examples from 2010, creating various shapes such as fish, leaves or conch shells. The moulds are made in either stone or wood and are around 2.5 to 5 cm (1 to 2 in) long. Although the *makha* can be shaped by hand into a simple ball, the idea of making a sweet take on the impression of a motif is where decoration and design meet. The notion of designing a mould to make a decorative dessert connects to the Hindu belief that absolutely all organic and inorganic materials, no matter how apparently insignificant, are intrinsic to religion and existence as a whole.

←

Saint Lamp

Date 2014
Designer Sahil & Sarthak
Materials Brass, rudraksha seeds

The process of hammering brass sheets by hand results in a subtle texture that celebrates the imperfections created by the human hand. Brassware artisans in Moradabad, Uttar Pradesh and in Old Delhi have worked with design duo Sahil & Sarthak to create the quaint Saint Lamp. The texture of the beads that wrap around the body of the hanging lamp complements the texture of the hammered brass, the shape of which is formed using a lathe. Inspired by objects carried by sadhus (holy ascetics) — the *kamandal* (page 50), which is a vessel based on the shape of gourds, and the *rudraksha mala* (page 54), which is a holy necklace made of *rudraksha* seeds — the Saint Lamp is a playful nod to the glow of spiritual enlightenment.

Khurja pottery

Date 1980s
Designer Unknown
Materials Khurja red clay,
feldspar, quartz

Like many crafts, the traditional Khurja pottery of western Uttar Pradesh is being replaced by a cheaper industrialized version and is on the verge of dying out. There is great potential, however, in blending Khurja handcraft techniques with mass-production. The city of Khurja in recent decades, for example, has become known as 'The Ceramics City', with approximately 500 industrial glazed-ceramic factories manufacturing objects such as toys, crockery and sanitary fittings. A small number of artisans who work in the traditional Khurja style from the fourteenth century still remain. These artisans hand-paint florals derived from Turko-Persian designs, and geometric shapes on objects such as vases, urns and planters. The pottery is first slip cast using a blend of the red clay of Khurja, feldspar and quartz, which is then glazed in a variety of colours such as blue, brown or orange.

←

Heritage™ Tiles

Date 1922
Designer Bharat Floorings
Materials Portland cement,
marble powder, natural pigment

Tiles from Bharat Floorings run through the hallways of the Chhatrapati Shivaji Terminus (CST) in Mumbai, walked through daily by millions of people. The Heritage™ range, seen here, replicate the famous Minton tiles that were brought into India by the British. In 1922 Pherozesha and Rustom Sidhwa founded Bharat and adapted their tile designs to suit Indian tastes, succeeding in halting the import of tiles from England. Each tile is handcrafted and the process begins with mixing white Portland cement, marble powder and natural colour pigments. The coloured mix is then poured into handmade metal moulds. A metal plate is placed over the top of each mould and the 10-mm (½-in) thick tile is pressed with a mechanical hydraulic press. Once removed from the moulds, they are placed on a rack until hard, after which they are left to cure in a tank of water for many days, hardening into concrete. This setting process leads to expansions, which result in tiny cracks that are part of the tiles' unique charm. Today, Bharat Floorings is working with young design studios, like The Busride and Bombay Duck Designs to formulate new local, contemporary designs.

←

Kanch ki churis

Date 2015
Designer Unknown
Materials Glass

Worn by women throughout the country, the clinking of these glass bangles is a familiar sound. Every city, town and village will have bangle sellers in markets and street vendors pushing their *thelas* (carts) full of colourful glass *churis*. Red *churis* are traditionally worn by Hindu women as a sign of marriage and green *churis* as a sign of *shringara* (meaning romantic or erotic love), as laid out in the historical nine *rasas*, or emotions, in Hindu aesthetics. Bare wrists are considered inauspicious. Should a woman become a widow, she will remove all jewellery forever and break the *churis* off her wrists. *Churis* are not exclusive to Hindu women, however, they are also a style accessory. The inexpensive, delicate bangles break so frequently that they are mass-produced in factories across the country, Firozabad, Uttar Pradesh being one of the largest industrial centres for *churi* making. The basic glass block is coloured, heated in a furnace and pieces are removed and shaped around spinning cone-shaped moulds. Plain or with decorative impressions and flecks of gold, *churis* are available in every colour imaginable and creating the perfect colour combination to match one's outfit is an art form.

Sajna Savarna

Mirror 6

Date 2015
Designer Spandana Gopal, Tiipoi
Materials Mirror alloy, cork, copper, shisham wood

Steeped in myth, spirituality and science, *Aranmula kannadi* (the craft of mirror making) was established in the village of Aranmula, Kerala. *Kannadis* (mirrors) — traditionally made with ornate, hand-cast brass frames — are considered auspicious and accompany marriage and religious ceremonies. Focusing on the technique rather than the decorative aspect, Spandana Gopal (b. 1985), founder of Tiipoi, has worked with a family that has been casting mirrors for eight generations, to create the world's largest *kannadi* with 'unfinished edges' mounted on copper. It took six attempts to create the final product. The process of casting the molten alloy in mud, using lost-wax casting, produces a 3 mm thick mirror, the surface of which is laboriously hand polished using oil and water, over the course of several days. Cotton cloth and velvet are used in the final stages in order to produce a flawless reflection. Unlike regular glass mirrors in which light is refracted from the back, the *kannadi* reflects light directly from its surface, which is considered to be more pure and worthy of the gods.

←

Kadla

Date Early twentieth century
Designer Unknown
Materials Silver alloy

These wide anklets, which are heavy despite being hollow (each weighs 980 g/2 lb), can be opened and closed by means of a screw. The circular part of the anklet rests on the back of the ankle while the more square-shaped segment is displayed at the front, resting on the top of the foot. Women from various communities in Gujarat wear such anklets, they are a common sight in the Saurashtra and Kutch regions. While some anklets feature detailed surface embellishments, the *kadla*, such as these early twentieth-century examples, are particularly abstract forms that visually dominate the ankle and foot. They are a symbol of wealth and so are intentionally worn with a *lehenga* (skirt) that ends at the mid-section of the calf.

←

Marble Bulbs

Date 2015
Designer Rooshad Shroff
Materials Makrana white marble, brass

Rooshad Shroff (b. 1983), a Mumbai-based architect, challenges the use of traditional materials and handcrafted techniques. Carved from Makrana white marble, his Marble Bulbs are a play on the traditional filament light bulb. The creation of this light fixture pushes to the extreme the limits of the craftsman, as each bulb is carved by hand from a single block of marble. The interior is then hollowed out on a lathe machine using a tool Shroff developed especially for the project. Finally, solid brass holders are hollowed out on the lathe and an LED fitted inside. The thinness of the marble is taken down to 6 mm (¼ in) so that the light can filter through. Inspired by cut-glass crystal, a range of over fifty different patterns have been made for the collection in varying shapes and sizes. The marble, which is quarried from around the town of Makrana in Rajasthan, is renowned for its translucent whiteness and is ideal for sculpting. It has been used for buildings such as the Taj Mahal and the Victoria Memorial of Kolkata.

Bahi-khata

Date 2015
Designer Unknown
Materials Cardboard, paper, cloth, thread, rope

These handmade account books have crimped pages that act as double-entry columns for those who know Mahajani, a mercantile accounting script believed to have been practised over centuries. Accountants needed two columns — one for debt (*naam*) and another for credit (*jama*) — and so craftsmen responded with this design. *Bahi-khata* are produced throughout India and are made by cutting yellow or white paper to the desired size and folding it into sections that are then handstitched through the spine of the red cloth and cardboard cover with a cotton rope. This rope is also used to wrap around the book and keep it secure. The red cover that invokes Lakshmi, the Hindu goddess of wealth and success, was originally handstitched but today is completed by machine — as are accounts themselves. Traditionally, new *bahi-khata* are purchased during the festival of Diwali to bring good luck and one can sometimes find towering piles of these in temples, at the feet of Lakshmi.

←

Channapatna toy

Date 2015
Designer Unknown
Materials Hale wood, lac

A series of small- and large-scale production factories that have been creating lacquered wooden toys since the nineteenth century are situated in Channapatna, a city located about 60 km (37 miles) southwest of Bangalore and popularly known as 'Toy Town'. Despite younger companies such as Gween Toys working with local artisans to make educational toys for a wider market, these toys will always be known locally as Channapatna toys. The *chitrakars* (craftsmen) use hale, which is a softwood with a tight grain. Various objects — including household goods, stationery and candlesticks, as well as toys — are finished in lacquer by turning the wood against a stick of lac (a resinous substance secreted by lac insects). The warmth created by the turning melts the lac, providing a rich coating of, often, primary colours. Finally, the lacquered objects are buffed with the leaves of the talegari (*Pandanus odoratissimus*), which gives them a lustrous shine.

←

Oxidized Brass Dokra Lights

Date 2013
Designer Manasa Prithvi, Ira Studio
Materials Brass

Dokra is a laborious and ancient craft of metal-casting practised in the tribal region of Bastar in Chhattisgarh and parts of western India. Using the lost-wax method, each mould is shaped and made using individual strips of beeswax, which are then handcast in brass or bell metal and given a black and gold oxidized finish. The simple form allows for the textural and handmade beauty of the mould to shine through. A black patina on the interior creates a soft ambience when lit. Dokra dates back many centuries, as evidenced by archaeological finds, but is still used today to create religious figures and utilitarian objects. Manasa Prithvi (b. 1989) of Ira Studio collaborated with Dokra artisans to produce this elegant set of lights and preserve this wonderful craft.

Sajna Savarna

Gobar kandhayi

Date 2015
Designer Unknown
Materials Cow dung, paper, gum, paint

The cow is considered sacred and useful in everyday Indian life. This notion includes the cow's dung, which is used to make toys. Cow dung is considered hygienic and, being available free of cost, is ideal for modelling into sculpture. Raghurajpur village and the cities of Puri and Bargarh in the state of Odisha are well known for these traditional *gobar* toys, which feature brightly coloured animal forms, birds, people and religious figures as common motifs. One way the toys are created is by covering an existing clay model of the desired form with layers of old paper moistened with water and gum. A string is placed between these layers, along the central horizontal axis of the model, and is gently pulled out once the papier mâché is dry, cutting the paper mould in half. This hollow mould is filled and reformed with cow dung and gum. The surface is then smoothed and painted in a base white followed by vividly coloured details.

←

Black pottery of Nizamabad

Date 2014
Designer Unknown
Materials Clay, *kabiz*

The whole town of Nizamabad, in the eastern part of Uttar Pradesh, is involved in the production of black pottery. It is believed that potters from Kutch, Gujarat, were brought here during the reign of the Mughal emperor Aurangzeb (1618–1707). The surface of the pottery is a lustrous black, typically inlaid with silver, although the example here is devoid of any embellishment. The clay, sourced from local ponds, is mixed with goat excrement, mango bark, and bamboo and adusa leaves, a mix known as *kabiz* that carbonizes when it is fired in the kiln. The kiln is fuelled by cow-dung patties and is completely closed, so that the resulting smoke imparts a black surface to the objects, which would otherwise be a reddish colour. The production costs related to making these pots are very low because everything is made using local, natural materials.

Namda rug

Date c. 1940s
Designer Unknown
Materials Cotton, wool

Simple and utilitarian felted wool rugs, *namdas* are used as mattresses and floor and wall coverings. They are handcrafted in Kashmir and are believed to have been introduced to the region in the twelfth century by Iranian travellers visiting India. The design is marked on a base fabric of heavy cotton or jute and the wool (some versions use a wool-cotton blend) felted onto it. *Namdas* are usually built up with a minimum of three layers of mostly mill-made carded wool, starting from the top layer and working down. Each layer of wool is spread, sprinkled with water and pressed with a tool known as a *pinjra* made of woven willow wicker. The mat is then rolled tightly for several hours and trodden on to squeeze out the water and bond the fibres. A final wash and dry completes the felted rug, which then serves as a base for floral and geometric *aari* (tambour hook) embroidery using wool or silk threads. This type of embroidery, which is characteristic of other Kashmiri textile arts, makes the *namdas* uniquely Kashmiri.

आना-जाना

Aana Jaana

Coming & Going

Hindustan Ambassador

Date Early 2000s
Designer Hindustan Motors
Materials Steel, rubber

The 'Amby', as it is affectionately known, is a car that is a symbol of Independence for Indians. There is a deeper attachment to this particular car, because it was the first to be produced post-Independence by Hindustan Motors, established by the Birla family as early as 1942. Production started in 1957 in the Uttarpara factory in West Bengal and the design and tooling were based on the Morris Oxford series III, with a semi-monocoque chassis and 1489cc engine. Spacious inside, it can fit two families on its wide bench seats with all the children sitting on the laps of the adults. It was *the* car until the Maruti (page 122) stole its thunder in the 1980s. The Ambassador is still, however, the choice for Delhi politicians, in white with a beacon light on the top, and it is still used as *kaali-peeli* (black-and-yellow) taxis in Delhi and yellow taxis in Kolkata. From Liberalization onwards, the Ambassador was forced to modernize — add power steering, even air-conditioning. People were misty-eyed upon hearing news of the abrupt factory closure in 2014, but it may go back into production, with a new, more futuristic, design.

←

Chai glasses and holder

Date 2015
Designer Unknown
Materials Glass, steel

Every day, students, office workers, taxi drivers and wage labourers gather around tea stalls throughout cities and railway stations for their much-treasured cup of hot chai. Chai, or tea, is made by brewing tea leaves with milk and sugar, sometimes with the addition of cloves, cardamom, black pepper, ginger or fennel. It is served in either clay *kulhads* (page 114) or these iconic chai glasses, which are around 9 cm (3½ in) in height, along with the metal holder used by the local *chaiwallah* (tea delivery peon). While plastic has, in many places, replaced glass, the design has remained consistent, with grooves down the side and a scalloped rim. Some are narrower at the bottom and some squatter, but all share the ease of stacking and washing for reuse, unlike the clay *kulhad* and the plastic cup, which are both disposed of after one use.

Cycle rickshaw

Date Early twentieth century
Designer Unknown
Materials Steel, rubber, PVC

The cycle rickshaw is a pedal tricycle with a carriage big enough to seat two people and a small overhead canopy. It is a low-cost means of transport suitable for people from all economic backgrounds and also provides employment for large numbers of *ricksha-wallahs* who manage to drive these rickety vehicles in all types of weather — from the arid cold winters to the searing hot summers. Believed to have been invented by an American missionary in Japan in the late 1800s, manually pulled rickshaws were used in parts of Shimla, Himachal Pradesh as early as 1880 and by the 1920s were being used by Chinese tradesmen in Kolkata. Today, the rickshaw is particularly effective in places like Chandni Chowk — the famous and incredibly busy market built by Shah Jahan in the 1600s. Here, one can find the oldest *attar* (perfume) and incense shops, a bird hospital, sweets, saris, books, religious paraphernalia, hardware, kitchen supplies and some of the best street food in Delhi. A hundred thousand cycle rickshaws, the highest number in Delhi, manoeuvre their way through the narrow, crowded alleys of Chandni Chowk alongside motorized two-wheelers.

Stunning Slippers Doormat

Date 2010s
Designer Krsna Mehta, India Circus
Materials Coir, rubber

Eighty-five per cent of coir doormats exported around the world are made in Kerala. They are made from the humble but versatile coconut, which yields a plethora of uses, including sustenance (water and food), fuel (shell), oil (kernel) and as a daily offering to Hindu gods and godesses. Among the many commercial products that are manufactured from the coconut, the fibrous husk — the coir or *kayar* (in Malayalam) — collected from between the exterior and the internal shell is used to make brushes, doormats and fillings for mattresses. The first factory to produce coir for floor mats was established in 1859 in Alleppey (Alappuzha), Kerala. The thick, waterproof coir is separated from the ripe coconut and twisted into yarn. The yarn is woven into rectangular mats on a handloom and the mats are cut and trimmed. Mats can be stencilled with decoration but most are left plain and undyed, or otherwise simply read 'welcome'. Krsna Mehta (b. 1979), product designer and artist, established India Circus to create products, such as this doormat, with striking graphics for a modern Indian look.

←

Codd Goli Soda Glass Bottles

Date 2015
Designer Hiram Codd
Materials Glass, marble, rubber

The Codd-neck bottle was designed in 1872 by Englishman Hiram Codd and was made specifically for carbonated drinks. Siddhivinayak Glass Concepts in Uttar Pradesh now manufacture and export the bottles but the design has remained the same, thus exemplifying the legacy of the British and the local adoption of such products. The special stopper — a small marble in the neck of the bottle, which is sealed with a rubber gasket — ensures that the drink is kept fizzy until opened. The neck has a pinch in it, which captures the marble after it is released from the gasket and prevents it from blocking the neck as the liquid is poured out. The bottle is filled upside down and this pressure forces the marble against the washer, thereby containing the carbonation. Although the designer may not be of Indian origin, the drink itself — *banta* or '*goli* (marble) soda' — is indigenous to north India and is sold primarily in Delhi, where street vendors display their rows of bottles with lemons placed on top. It can be served with ice, masala, lemon juice or *kala namak* (black salt) and is extremely popular.

←

Pani puri cart

Date Early twenty-first century
Designer Unknown
Materials Wood, glass

The iconic pani puri cart comprises rectangular boxes made of wood and glass fixed to a cart (*thela*), which serves as a mobile snack station. Each box has a series of compartments, within which are stored all the ingredients to make pani puri — the beloved street snack. No pani puri cart is exactly the same, all have small variations, although a typical distinction is that some have one level of boxes and others have two. The key is that the street vendor can easily move the unit to as many different locations as possible, thereby creating more business. The vendor stands behind the cart on one side, where he prepares pani puri (also known as *golgappa* or *puchka*). The puffed biscuit (puri) is filled with chickpeas, potatoes and chilled spiced water (pani), and topped with tamarind chutney. Because dinner is often eaten after 9 p.m., a quick evening snack of pani puri on the way home is part of a tradition of street culture.

Fire buckets

Date Early 2000s
Designer Unknown
Materials Galvanized steel

Brightly painted red fire buckets made of galvanized steel originated in the British era and are still commonly used, as fire emergency services are not always able to reach a fire, especially in densely populated or tight urban spaces. The series of buckets filled with sand hangs on a simple rack. The bright colour and word 'FIRE' painted in large block letters make their use obvious to onlookers or passers-by in the case of an emergency. The ubiquitous buckets can be found at petrol stations, museums and outside of shops and are one of the vestiges of colonialism.

Bajaj Chetak scooter

Date 1980s
Designer Bajaj Auto Limited
Materials Steel, rubber

The loveable Chetak is still seen zipping through congested traffic, often with a whole family aboard — husband driving, wife seated holding a newborn baby and young son standing in the front — regardless of new developments like the Tata Nano city car, aimed at weaning people off two-wheeled transport. *Hamara Bajaj*, or 'Our Bajaj' was a reliable, economical form of transport and could get up to 80 km/h (50 mph). The design was licensed on the Vespa in 1972 until the 1980s when it was remodelled by a Bajaj in-house designer. It was fully manufactured in India by Bajaj Auto company until 2009 when production ceased because of intense competition from the many imports that began to flood the country post-Liberalization. The scooter is an icon of the middle class moving from socialism to capitalism. It was named Chetak in honour of Maharana Pratap Singh's horse. Singh was a Rajput warrior who battled the Mughals in the late 1500s. Like a trusted horse, the scooter photographed here belongs to a local tailor in Bandra, who can no longer get parts for it, but claims it still rides like a dream.

Atlas Roadster bicycle

Date 2000s
Designer Atlas Cycles
Materials Steel, rubber

The Atlas Roadster, a city bicycle, has been in production since 1951 and was first introduced by the late Rai Bahadur Shri Janki Das Kapur (1893–1967), who established the Atlas Cycles factory in Sonipat, Haryana, in 1951. Despite the founding of Hero Cycles a few years later, by the four Munjal brothers, Atlas Cycles became one of the largest manufacturers in Asia and began exporting in 1958. The bicycles — both new and old ones made rickety through use — are found everywhere, including parts of Africa and South America. The Roadster model, based on the British roadster, sports a distinctive cut-out in the steel chainring that reads 'Atlas'. This utility bike has one gear, rod brakes, cotter pin cranks and weighs a hefty 18 kg (40 lb). It costs about 3,000 rupees (around £30) and is used to transport all manner of goods, including cloth, food, lengthy steel pipes and milk jugs — always in towering piles that appear too heavy but that the weight of the bike manages to counterbalance.

Bata Tennis shoes

Date 2015
Designer Bata Brands
Materials Canvas, rubber

Although the product and design of a Czech company, the iconic white canvas tennis shoe has long been part of most school uniforms in India. Originally created for physical education classes, it has been in production at the same factory in Batanagar, near Kolkata, since 1934. These unisex shoes, which sell today for about 500 rupees (around £5) a pair, still retain their distinctive green stripe running along the white rubber trim, their elongated shape and their ribbed toe guard. The special contour was designed in order to fit all shapes and sizes of feet across the country. White canvas shoes are stipulated by most schools, who always specify (in brackets) 'Bata Tennis shoes'. In 2014 they were re-launched for the Western market, in fashionable concept stores such as Colette in Paris or Dover Street Market in London. This reincarnation was manufactured using better-quality canvas and rubber, producing a shoe that millions of school kids, who habitually rubbed white chalk over black scuffs, could never imagine.

Kulhad

Date 2015
Designer Unknown
Materials Terracotta

The finest example of a biodegradable and disposable utensil is the *kulhad*, a small terracotta cup, such as this example from 2015, that is thrown and smashed upon the ground after just one use. Their inherent sterile nature comes from the high temperatures at which they are fired. However, for hygiene purposes, they are not recycled. The tradition of making clay cups dates back some 5,000 years to the Indus Valley Civilization. *Kulhads* come in various shapes and sizes and can be handmade or machine made. They are used for serving tea, yogurt, lassi (churned yogurt), kulfi or *thandai* (a popular cold drink). As tea is poured into a *kulhad*, part of the liquid is absorbed into the unglazed clay, giving a distinctively earthy taste that cannot be replicated with plastic cups, now primarily used for the serving of tea. Former Minister Lalu Prasad Yadav (b. 1948) tried to revitalize the use of clay cups in railway stations and on trains in 2004, for environmental reasons, but was met with criticism and the difficulty of supplying the 1.8 billion *kulhads* needed per year.

Istri

Date 2013
Designer Unknown
Materials Wood, iron, aluminium

Come rain or shine, in neighbourhoods countrywide, one can be sure to find an *istriwallah* or *presswallah* outside ironing and folding clothes. The *istri* looks as if it is straight out of the nineteenth century, which is quite accurate, as these flat irons have remained pretty much unchanged since then. Manufactured in brass, iron or aluminium with a heavy wooden handle, the coal-filled irons weigh 7 to 10 kg (15 to 22 lb). Brass *istri* are the best for pressing but are also the heaviest, and iron *istri* rust quickly, so aluminium is a popular choice, as it is lightweight and the least expensive. The *istriwallah* or *dhobi* (washerman or washerwoman) will come to one's home to pick up clothes and return them shortly after, in neatly pressed stacks bundled in cloth. *Istri* are a means of mobile self-employment requiring very few resources. Many urban households keep electric irons for last minute touch-ups but the majority of their pressing is done by the local *istriwallah*.

Ice gola machine

Date 2000s
Designer Amir Rajkot
Materials Cast iron

A *gola* is a dessert of shaved ice that is served with a cup full of sweet and sour syrup for dipping. The *golawallah*, or *gola* hawker, will stand for hours at his *thela* (cart), operating the ice *gola* machine and using a little bell and several bottles of colourful concentrated syrups to attract the attention of customers. A large block of ice sits between two plates of metal in the manually operated machine. One plate presses down on top of the ice block, forcing it onto a thin plate with a sharp-bladed gap in its centre. As the *golawallah* turns the wheel, perfect slivers of ice are shaved off and collected underneath. The shavings are transferred into a cup, which has already been filled with syrup, such as orange, lemon or *kala khatta* (jamun, a blackberry-type fruit), or is moulded onto a popsicle stick and dipped into the cup of syrup. This sticky delight is consumed throughout the day but mostly in the evening, when the air is slightly cooler and people come out for their walks.

←

Tea kettle

Date 2005
Designer Unknown
Materials Brass

Chai is the hot beverage that fuels the majority of Indians. As a start to one's morning, as a social drink accompanied by some conversation or as a late afternoon jolt, hot, sweet, milky chai can be found anywhere, any time and the *chaiwallah* is always happy to make another cup for you. Chai stalls are an essential part of the landscape and can be found by the roadside, in a stall, under a tree, or as the mobile version — *chaiwallahs* walking the streets, with their iconic kettle in one hand and cups or *kulhads* (page 114) in the other, announcing, 'Chai, garam garam chai' (tea, hot hot tea). With much dexterity, the *chaiwallah* manages to pour the tea and hold the cups while simultaneously taking your money! The aluminium or brass kettle, locally pronounced 'kat-lee', is derived from a traditional British kettle design and has a gooseneck spout, lid and handle.

Nilkamal moulded plastic chairs

Date Early 2000s
Designer Nilkamal Limited
Materials Plastic

No other furniture in recent times has revolutionized how people sit more than the Nilkamal moulded plastic chair. These lightweight, durable and affordable chairs can be seen everywhere from homes, offices, schools, hospitals, eateries, cricket matches and wedding functions to the solitary broken plastic chair by the roadside. Founded in the 1930s, Nilkamal started out producing buttons and diversified over the years into plastics and in the 2000s their moulded plastic chairs began to enter the market. From the humble stackable chair in various colours to more ornate plastic sofa sets mimicking carved wood, there is an affordable design available for everyone.

←

Coffee tumbler and davara

Date 2015
Designer Unknown
Materials Stainless steel

Madras *kaapi* (coffee) is served in a stainless-steel tumbler and a squat stainless-steel bowl with a wide lip, known as a *davara*, such as the modern examples seen here. Coffee is poured into the tumbler and then transferred back and forth between the *davara* and the tumbler to both cool and aerate it, creating a nice froth and evenly distributing the sugar and the milk. It is also called 'metre coffee' because of the long distance held between the two vessels when pouring. Finally, the coffee is sipped from the *davara*. Madras coffee is sweet and milky, made from dark-roasted coffee beans and chicory that is then mixed with frothy boiled milk. The decoction involves a particular preparation, using a specific coffee filter that very slowly filters the coffee grounds and chicory. This type of coffee is common in the southern Indian states and is drunk throughout Andhra Pradesh, Karnataka, Kerala and Tamil Nadu where there are abundant coffee plantations.

←

Maruti 800

Date 1990s
Designer Maruti Suzuki India Limited
Materials Steel, rubber

The history of this resilient city car begins in the early 1970s when former Prime Minister Indira Gandhi (1917–1984) and her government proposed the establishment of a private company to research, develop and manufacture what could be a totally indigenous car, and also a 'People's Car', during a period of a closed import market. With the help of Sanjay Gandhi (1946–1980), Indira's son, Maruti Udyog Limited was established and a decade later a licensing deal with the Suzuki Motor Company was signed. Suzuki provided their Alto model as a design reference and in 1983 the Maruti 800 was produced with an 800cc engine, giving it its name. The car was manufactured in Gurgaon, Haryana and marked an automobile revolution in India, as it was the first car to be wholly produced with local parts. Over 2.87 million were produced, 2.66 million of which were sold within India, before production ceased in 2014. Many are still seen on the streets, zooming around with determined presence.

Meerut Barber Scissors

Date 2010
Designer Meerut community
Materials Scrap metal

In 2013 the scissors produced in Meerut, Uttar Pradesh were given the geographical indicator (GI) tag. GI status is given to goods that have an association with a particular location, like Darjeeling tea or Benares brocade, and helps prevent fraudulent replicas. Meerut has been producing barber, tailor and paper scissors entirely from scrap metal purchased from automobile and railway industries since the seventeenth century. The metal is heated and hammered by hand then flattened into plates with roller machines. The barber scissors are lightweight and made from a single piece of metal. The blades, which are short and can be opened and shut quickly, are made using an old mould-casting process and great precision is used for riveting and grinding. A popular saying, referring to Meerut barber scissors lasting for generations, is 'grandfather buys, grandson uses'.

Ghantadi

Date 2015
Designer Lohar caste
Materials Scrap iron, copper powder, wood

These bells, made entirely from recycled metals, are designed to meet the needs of nomadic herdsmen crossing back and forth between Sindh (now in Pakistan) and the Kutch district of Gujarat. They have been made for centuries, based on a highly skilled craft developed by bell makers (from the Lohar caste) together with herdsmen. Entire families are involved in the making process: while men beat strips of iron into a cylindrical shape, women carry out the finishing, submerging the iron bell into a mixture of mud and water, and then covering it with a copper powder that adheres to the mud mixture. Flattened pieces of cotton, which are presoaked in the mixture, are wrapped around the bell's exterior. After baking in a small oven, the excess mud and cotton are removed to reveal a copper-coloured surface that has an inherent patina. The bells come in thirteen different sizes and are dented using a hammer-like tool called an *ekalavai*, which gives each bell its own particular *vaaji* (tone). In each size, up to six different tones can be created to distinguish the different animals and the owners of cattle.

←

Buxa

Date 2011
Designer Unknown
Materials Aluminium

On the streets, in homes, on railway cars, buses and taxis, wherever you go in India, you will see *buxa*. They are a democratic storage system used by both the wealthy and the poor and are greatly symbolic of migration and transport. *Buxa* have been used by artists to speak about the trauma and memory of the Partition of India in 1947, where millions of people rapidly threw their belongings into such trunks before leaving their homes for good. The lightweight trunks are still made of aluminium with hard, rounded corners and come in a variety of sizes. They also have clasps for attaching external locks. Aluminium, which has only been used for the last 150 years, is made from the raw material, bauxite, which is found throughout central India.

Autorickshaw

Date 2015
Designer Bajaj Auto Limited
Materials Sheet metal, PVC

The noisy, sputtering sound of an autorickshaw is familiar to inhabitants of most cities in India. The rickshaw, originally designed by Corradino D'Ascanio for Piaggio in 1947, is called the Ape (Italian for 'bee'), the companion to the Vespa ('wasp') by the same designer, although it is known by many other names across Asia. The vehicle is a great example of early global market trade, being imported to India by former Prime Minister Jawaharlal Nehru in 1952 who was attracted by Piaggio's licensing deal and export strategy. This three-wheeled vehicle was designed to carry cargo in post-war Italy, but in India serves as an affordable taxi that can travel up to 80 km/h (50 mph). Currently produced by Bajaj Auto Ltd, the rickshaw has either a two-stroke engine with a lever that is pumped to get started, or a four-stroke engine that simply requires the turn of a key. This model runs on compressed natural gas (CNG) so it can be prone to sticky situations — hence why it comes equipped with a fire extinguisher. As a mobile form of advertising, it can publicize everything from the latest Bollywood film releases to an anti-honking campaign.

←

Hawai chappals

Date 2011
Designer Relaxo Footwears Limited
Materials Rubber

Rubber footwear became incredibly popular in India because rubber is waterproof and heat resistant — perfect for Indian weather. The light-blue-and-white *hawai chappals* (flip-flops) are worn daily by young and old. They are cheap, handy slip-ons commonly worn throughout the day. They are ubiquitous and can be spotted on the feet of many city dwellers who are running errands, playing cricket, driving rickshaws in hot weather, or walking through monsoon-flooded alleyways.

Milk churn

Date 2000s
Designer Unknown
Materials Steel

India is currently the largest producer and consumer of milk in the world, with over 100 million tonnes produced a year and demand is growing. Used for making paneer, butter, yogurt, *mithai*, kulfi, *chaas* or buttermilk, it is India's top commodity, matching the combined value of rice and wheat. Given this level of output, milk is sourced by both public and private sectors. It is available in Tetra Pak containers or small sealed plastic bags but the majority is still delivered in traditional milk churns or cylindrical steel cans. Now a vintage item in the West, the milk churn is used daily to transport milk from dairy farms to the cities for wider distribution. Made of welded non-corrosive steel, which keeps the milk cooler than aluminium does, and with welded handles, the large canisters are seen swinging on the outside of trains and on either side of a Hero or Atlas bicycle (page 114). The milk is transported in unrefrigerated, open-air conditions and so must be sourced and consumed daily.

Weighing scales

Date c. 1970s
Designer Unknown
Materials Iron, steel

So many things in India function perfectly without depending on electricity, which can be scarce in rural areas, small towns and poorer urban neighbourhoods. An entire ecosystem of individual shops, merchants and street vendors throughout the country conducts its daily business using these scales. Unpackaged fresh foods and bulk items are sold by metric weight using portable weighing scales with cast-iron hexagonal weights. Jewellers will use precision scales and bullion weights when trading in precious metals. Electric scales are readily available but the classic non-electric ones are more accessible for the larger population. In 1957 India, with its own unique history of weights and measurements, dropped the British imperial system and adopted the metric system.

Premier Padmini

Date 1990s
Designer Fiat
Materials Steel, rubber

Mumbai's famous black-and-yellow taxis were originally Fiats that were licensed to India in 1952. The car was launched by Premier Automobiles (now Premier Ltd) and sold as a Fiat 1100 until 1973, when it was produced locally and renamed Premier Padmini. Production ceased in 2000 and the demise of the Padmini can be traced to 1991 and the liberalization of the economy, which allowed foreign manufacturers to set up production within India and increased competition. These four-door saloons, with bench seats in the front and back, are now slowly being retired since the local city government has voiced concerns about pollution. With its disappearance will also vanish the sensation of entering your own disco party — complete with lighting, mirrors, images of gods, all kinds of signage and music — together with an equally nonconformist driver. The loss of this iconic car led designer Sanket Avlani to create the start-up company Taxi Fabric, a unique platform for artists and illustrators to create custom tapestries that decorate the interiors of taxis and keep up the lively character of the city of Mumbai.

Royal Enfield Motorcycle

Date 2010s
Designer Royal Enfield
Materials Steel, rubber

The Enfield Cycle Company was founded in the late 1800s in Worcestershire, England, and produced motorcycles under the licensed brand name 'Royal Enfield', but was eventually dissolved in 1971. Sixteen years prior to its closure, however, Enfield had partnered with Madras Motors to establish Enfield India in Chennai, which remains open to this day. The Royal Enfield Bullet, with its 350cc engine, was originally imported to India for use by police officers and the army to patrol the borders. In 1957, however, Enfield India began manufacturing and producing the famous Bullet motorcycle and even exported it to Europe. Today, the company is known as Royal Enfield and exports to over 40 countries, including Japan and Argentina. The motorcycle seen here is the Classic 350 model. Enfield has relaunched the iconic Bullet with a 500cc engine, twin spark ignition and better fuel usage. No longer associated with the police or army, the mid-weight bike is now affordable and accessible.

←

Dabba

Date 2015
Designer Aristo Steel
Materials Stainless steel

Barrelling down the street on a bicycle in the heat of mid-afternoon, is a *dabbawallah* returning empty *dabbas* (or tiffins) to Churchgate station in Mumbai. From this railway station, the tiffins will be returned to their homes in the suburbs. The next morning, fresh food will be cooked, the tiffin will be filled and delivered, along with 200,000 others, to office workers in the city. Started by Mahadeo Havaji Bachche, the tradition of tiffin delivery began in 1890, in response to the rapid growth of workers entering the city. The tiffin is a series of three or four containers that stack on top of each other and are held together by two external latches, which are secured along the top of the handle. Its design is a throwback to *sherpai*, or measuring bowls, and its name stems from the word 'tiffin', which was introduced by the British, meaning to have a light snack in between meals. Originally made in brass (giving the food a better texture and taste) and enamel, today it is made primarily in stainless steel, like this example from Aristo Steel. Contents include vegetables, daal, roti, pickles and rice. Miraculously, it all stays warm.

←

Kolhapuri chappals

Date 2015
Designer Chamar community
Materials Buffalo hide, cotton

An indigenous flat-soled leather sandal with a loop for the big toe, the *Kolhapuri chappal* — from the city of Kolhapur in Maharashtra — is made by the Chamar community and is a unisex and affordable shoe, making it a design classic. Since the 1990s, government efforts to update and promote the industry have ensured their widespread use. Made from buffalo and goat hides that are tanned naturally with vegetable dyes ranging from light beige to dark brown, the *chappals* are cut, stitched and glued by hand. Their beauty lies in the intricately stamped leatherwork and the finely braided leather strips. Design details include characteristic 'ear flaps' or *kaan* that are attached to sides of the instep band, small decorative red pompoms or gold braided thread and metal eyelets applied to the leatherwork. While the open toe-ring and strap style is the traditional design, the shoe's popularity has encouraged other stylistic variations such as woven closed-toe slippers and an extensive range of bright colours.

Kangri

Date 2013
Designer Shaksaz
Materials Willow, earthenware

The *kangri* is a portable heater, that is carried close to the body, under the *pheran* (oversized coat), for use both inside and outside of the home. It is used in Kashmir during the cold winters, in homes that lack any other kind of heating. A willow basket holds an earthenware pot in which coal and chinar leaves are kept sparking with the aid of a metal spatula. After gathering the willow, which was first employed for this use in the nineteenth century, it is boiled and dried, giving it a nice, deep-brown shade, as well as making it pliant for weaving. The outer skin comes off during the boiling and the remaining inside is cleaned and cut into 5-mm (¼-in) strips. The weaving of the *kangri* is multi-directional and can include dyed green or bright pink strips, for a more colourful design. The *kangris* are primarily made in the town of Charari Sharief (Jammu and Kashmir) by the *shaksaz*, or basket makers.

←

Bhel puri stand

Date 2014
Designer Unknown
Materials Cane, plastic

The concept of a mobile snack station is inherent in the design of the classic bhel puri stand, with its lightweight base in the shape of a drum. Constructed from cane and tied together with recycled plastic, there is also a shoulder strap included so that the hawker can move his equipment from place to place. This ingenious design is the inspiration for Sian Pascale/Young Citizens' Bhel Puri side table (page 274). The mobile snack station serves *chaat* – a variety of savoury snacks that include fried crispy flat biscuits, puffed rice with lentils, chutneys and onions. The hawker has several little containers for all the different ingredients and when he moves from one area to another he balances the steel plate on top of his head while putting the stand over his shoulder.

←

Paduka, Kharawan, Karom

Date 2015
Designer Unknown
Materials Wood, varnish

Minimal footwear that is associated with mendicants and with the holy footprints of certain deities, the traditional *paduka* is a simple wooden board roughly cut to the shape of a footprint. It has a post that is designed for gripping between the big toe and second toe. *Padukas* suit a mendicant's simple way of life, wandering from place to place. They are comfortable in the extreme climate and also offer protection from the ground, which can get very hot. The *padukas* shown here are flat, but often there are platforms at the toe and heel of the soles to raise one's feet off the ground. Although generally associated with sadhus and religious teachers, highly decorative *padukas* made from precious materials are worn by high-status individuals, such as royalty and holy men, and are even given to some brides as part of their trousseau. This variety bear ornate work such as inlay, repoussé and carvings, depicting stylized motifs such as fish and hourglasses.

Handcart or Hathgadi

Date 2011
Designer Unknown
Materials Wood

Alongside the hundreds of cars, trucks, buses and bicycles, one will spot a handcart, towering with cargo, being pushed through the traffic by two men sweating profusely. Even in a busy city like Mumbai, impatient drivers slow down to allow them to pass. The handcart is heavy, but is an incredibly simple construction of two wheels on either side of recycled wooden planks, based on carts that trace their origins back to the Indus Valley Civilization. It is all rather hastily put together, and yet reliably strong. Used to transport anything from steel pipes and sugar cane to hundreds of tiffins, the handcarts and their drivers play an instrumental part in Indian street life, including transporting the wounded in emergencies and providing a spot for weary drivers to take a post-lunch nap. Under civic law, every handcart is numbered to match the driver's licence.

Tabletop telephone

Date 2015
Designer Unknown
Materials Plastic

Although it seems that nearly everyone has a mobile phone and a satellite dish in the post-Liberalized economy of India, there are those who still rely on this line-powered telephone. It accepts one rupee coins and is reliable regardless of power surges, which occur often. This phone is now replacing the yellow wall-mounted option found in PCOs, or Public Call Offices, that were introduced in the 1990s to both urban and rural environments. It says on the phone, 'A perfect choice', but its use is less about choice and more about necessity.

Bombay horn

Date c. 1930s
Designer Unknown
Materials Brass, rubber

Various large vehicles in India have the kitschy and catchy phrase 'Horn OK Please' — which should really read 'Horn Please, OK' — painted on the back, alerting other drivers to honk before they overtake. Prior to the automated horn, which has now led to a culture of incessant honking and the use of some fancy melodic tunes, there was the Bombay horn. This is a brass horn, with a rubber bulb (initially used in France when automobiles first came into production in the late nineteenth century) that makes a distinctive double honk sound. The horns are now sold as antiques but they are still used on autorickshaws in cities such as Ahmedabad, Gujarat or Jaipur, Rajasthan.

←

Sandwich toaster

Date 2015
Designer Unknown
Materials Aluminium

This aluminium sandwich toaster is used for making the iconic Bombay sandwich. Popular with college students and office workers alike, the affordable toasted sandwich is a delicious lunch or snack found on street stalls. The bread is buttered, then filled with vegetables such as cucumber, beetroot, onions and boiled potatoes, and sprinkled with *chaat masala*. The secret of the Bombay sandwich's success is the mint and coriander chutney that is spread over the salted butter, an ingredient so popular that Natco Foods Ltd even sells its own prepared Bombay Sandwich Spread in a jar. The sandwich is put inside the hinged toaster, which is then placed over coals to give a perfect smoky flavour. The handles are long so that the street hawker can safely keep his hands at some distance from the heat.

←

Lorry

Date 2015
Designer Unknown
Materials Steel, rubber

Millions of lorries transport goods across the country, carrying raw materials and industrial products wrapped in cloth and secured with ropes. The sight of an astoundingly oversized load balanced precariously on the back of a speeding lorry is both disarming and humorous. The drivers have a dangerous job and so they have the exterior and interior of the cabs heavily decorated with images of gods and hands in prayer and hang black cotton tassels from the back flaps and rearview mirrors to keep away bad spirits. The horns of the lorries are often very melodious and each lorry announces its presence and reflects its individuality through the sound of its horn and its elaborately painted decorations.

आराम करना
Aaraam Karna

Relaxing

Damroo Stool

Date 2013
Designer IndiaUrban
Materials Steel, cotton

This contemporary stool is a delightful example of handcrafted tradition for the twenty-first century. Its shape is inspired by the *damru* — the double-headed hand drum — and the *mooda* stool (page 168). Handcrafted from a light mild steel with a handwoven top in either cotton, jute or plastic, the stool is part of the Damroo furniture series. Easy to move around, its use is integral to the Indian way of life of spontaneous gatherings, conversations and drinking chai. It is suited to seamless indoor and outdoor living, whether on verandahs, balconies, rooftops or in courtyards and within the home.

Bombay Bunai Kursi

Date 2013
Designer Sian Pascale, Young Citizens
Materials Steel, plastic, timber

Sian Pascale is an Australian designer and founder of Young Citizens design studio, who worked in Mumbai for a few years, articulating a local language of design that could be understood as both nostalgic and forward-thinking. The Bombay Bunai Kursi is easily stackable, made from a light, powder-coated, hollow-steel frame, woven-plastic seating and handmade timber feet. Working with local weavers, who use cane, plastic or wicker, the art of *bunai* (weaving) was adapted to create this limited range of seating that utilizes hand processes and contemporary design solutions. The Bombay Bunai Kursi was originally designed for Kombava Café at The Art Loft (now closed) in Bandra, a suburb of Mumbai that has a concentration of artists, actors, designers and writers.

←

Planter's chair

Date Mid- to late twentieth century
Designer Unknown
Materials Rosewood

As its name suggests, this is the chair used by those working on plantations, for resting after a long, gruelling day. It was also popular among the British, unaccustomed to the heat of the colonies, to put up their feet. The genius of this chair is that, under each armrest, is a plank of wood that swivels outwards to the perfect length for resting legs. By the mid-nineteenth century these chairs were being exported out of India and were included in the 'Barrack Furniture and Camp Equipment' section of the 1907 Army & Navy Stores catalogue in two styles: the 'Indian Chair' with a teak frame and cane seat; and 'The Watherston', which had a green canvas-slung seat. The origins of the Planter's chair design are unclear, although its sloping back and axis are similar to the Campeche chair (introduced by the Spanish) and the Butaque chair (found in Mexico and in Sri Lanka). Nevertheless, it is a product that marries influences from the East and the West. The Planter's chair was made for use on verandahs in either cane, teak or rosewood.

The Indian subcontinent is an amalgamation of peoples, cultures, languages and philosophies. Throughout history, Indian culture has been subject to myriad influences, from the Mughal Empire to the British Raj to the now globalized nation in transition. *Sār: The Essence of Indian Design* takes readers on a journey across this diverse country, discovering everyday Indian objects from antiquity to the present day.

Explore the elements that make Indian design so special, from the techniques of the country's longstanding and incredibly skilled artisans to the ongoing responses to nature and necessity from contemporary designers and NGOs.

A perceptive introduction explores the development of an Indian identity and language for design that was encouraged by nationalists from Mahatma Gandhi to Jawaharlal Nehru and Western designers Charles and Ray Eames. With striking photography and informative captions, *Sār* – or 'essence' in Hindi – encapsulates Indian design through 200 objects, ranging from classics including the Hindustan Ambassador and the tiffin, to appropriated objects such as the autorickshaw and *hawai chappals*, alongside innovative contemporary pieces from both established and up-and-coming design studios such as Tiipoi, Wrap and Raw Mango.

Φ

Sarota

Date Twentieth century
Designer Unknown
Materials Brass

The betel nut is one of the main components of *paan* – a combination of betel nut, betel leaf and sometimes tobacco, which is chewed as a stimulant or mouth freshener and can be highly addictive. The betel nut, or *supari*, which grows on areca palms (*Areca catechu*) along the coastal regions of India, is cut with a *sarota*. The traditional hinged *sarota* fits neatly into the curve of the hand and features a sharp blade. It can be made from brass, steel or iron and is hand-cast, allowing for a range of shapes and sizes, from simple and affordable floral designs to more complex human and animal forms. A particular favourite motif is the bird, as seen here, owing to the wing-like motion as you cut the betel nut. More ornate *sarotas* feature couples in a state of embrace, as chewing *paan* is, for many, a sensual and leisurely experience. The culture of chewing *paan* dates back to ancient India and this fine brass example of a *sarota* was probably owned by an elite member of society.

Chillum

Date 2015
Designer Unknown
Materials Clay

Images of sadhus (holy ascetics) smoking *charas* (hashish or marijuana) in *chillums* are common depictions used to convey the exotic side of India. A *chillum* comprises a slightly flared pipe or funnel and a smaller conical-shaped 'stone' made of the same material. The stone sits in the wider end of the pipe and acts as a stopper or support for the substance being smoked. The *chillum* should not be touched by the mouth and is cupped by both hands in a particular way so that smoke inhalation is more direct. Made from stone, clay, glass or wood, designs range from minimal styles to ones with elaborate carvings of Shiva, Ganesha or Om. Sadhus commonly announce 'boom shankar' or 'boom shiva' before smoking, to let Shiva know they are about to smoke and invite other sadhus to join them, ultimately for a closer connection to the divine. *Chillums* are not just used by holy people but by all who enjoy the act of smoking hashish or marijuana, which has taken place in India since Vedic times.

←

Wrap Bench

Date 2013
Designer Ayush Kasliwal, AKDPL
Materials Metal, acacia wood, jute

Ayush Kasliwal's Wrap Bench celebrates furniture with a minimal and sustainable footprint and is inspired by two indigenous designs of India – the *charpai* (page 184) and the bullock cart – as well as modern Western design. The frame is made of acacia wood, over which unprocessed jute cord is wrapped to create the seating surface, similar to a *charpai*. Two small, cross-shaped metal braces support the two ends of the bench and provide additional strength, taking their cue from the bullock cart. Acacia is a native Indian wood known for its strength and is often used in the making of bullock carts and *charpais*. Jute, also known as hessian or 'golden fibre', is a vegetable fibre from the *Corchorus* plant that is highly sought after for its strength, lustre and versatility. Kasliwal studied at the National Institute of Design and works with local craftsmen to revive historical techniques.

Patra

Date c.1940s
Designer Unknown
Materials Silver

The *patra* is a very low stool used in the kitchen. Although it is traditionally made from wood, this example from the 1940s is made from silver and was part of the household items belonging to a bridal trousseau. In the same way that much of the Indian way of life is about sitting, eating or working directly on the floor, the *patra* is a stool onto which a woman, working in the kitchen, can squat or rest her haunches. Most kitchens have a little stool like this stowed away in a corner, standing vertically to take up as little space as possible in a room that is characteristically small or narrow, with low granite counters and wooden cabinets.

Ganjifa playing cards

Date 2010
Designer Sudha Venkatesh
Materials Watercolour, gum arabic, gold leaf and varnish on paper

The origins of *ganjifa* playing cards can be traced to Persia and were first popularized by Mughal rulers in the sixteenth century. The word *ganj* means treasure. The term *ganjifa* covers a variety of card games, and the cards themselves — which are either circular or rectangular — traditionally feature themes that are religious or social in nature. They are hand-painted by artisans on base materials such as leather, sandalwood, palm and birch leaf, mica, ivory and paper, using mostly natural colours of red, green, blue and yellow. Gesso, or a mixture of plaster and glue, is applied on some parts over which gold foil is laid. The nineteenth century ruler of Mysore, Krishnaraja Wadiyar III, created a set of cards called *kalyana ganjifa*, which conveyed leisure, elegance and relationships. *Ganjifa* artist Sudha Venkatesh (b. 1952), inspired by Wadiyar's *kalyana ganjifa*, created her own set, which we see here, depicting a modern-day Hindu wedding ceremony in South India. The work plays on the idea of pairing in relationships, card games and Indian and European cultures.

←

El'bo Stool

Date 2009
Designer Garima Roy
Materials Bamboo, cane, glue

The late Professor M.P. Ranjan, who taught at the National Institute of Design from 1974 onwards, was an avid believer in the endless uses of bamboo and worked with tribal communities in northeast India in order to revive its role in craft and industry. He also worked with students and craftsmen to develop a wider understanding of how bamboo, due to it being an extremely fast-growing plant and a natural composite, could become one of India's key materials and a part of sustainable craft. Designer Garima Roy, a former student of Ranjan, developed this contemporary stool using bamboo splints that were heated and bent to the required shape, after which they were glued back to back, providing strength. The inner surface is painted and the stool's legs are secured with cane binding. The seating surface includes half-lap joints, which bring the three sections together in a simple construction.

समय | अधिकारी
6.AM.TO2.P.M. | रविवार
| शुक्रवार
10.P.M.to6.A.M. | रविवार
रिलिवर | बुधवार

Chatai

Date 2010s
Designer Unknown
Materials Plastic

Modern and colourful plastic *chatai* are inspired by traditional Persian, Mughal-style carpets. Inexpensive, durable, soft and readily available in most markets the mats feature florals, geometrics and, sometimes, religious imagery. They are woven with plastic 'threads' or 'cords' using jacquard looms. Recycled plastic is also used. So much of India's seating culture remains on the ground — sleeping, sitting, praying or eating — and in the past, hand-loom carpets, rugs and mats would have been used. However, recycled plastic is a more affordable and environmentally friendly option.

←

Mooda

Date 2014
Designer Unknown
Materials Plastic, rubber

Shaped like a drum, the *mooda* is a traditional low stool. It would have been one of the select pieces of furniture, other than the ceremonial throne, used for seating and people would have sat cross-legged on it, placing the whole body on the surface. Very versatile, the *mooda* was also used by the British as a table, as a chair and, often, as a footstool. It is commonly made from bamboo and the stalk of the sarkanda plant, with two circles at the top and bottom, and two layers of strips wrapped diagonally in a criss-cross pattern between them. *Mooda* are found throughout the country, but are most famously produced in Haryana, where the sarkanda plant (*Saccharum bengalense*) grows in abundance. This particular, more modern, example was found in Assam and is made with a recycled tyre for the base and, instead of bamboo, plastic is the main material.

←

Cane chair

Date Early 1900s
Designer Chinese carpenters in Calcutta
Materials Wood, cane

By the middle of the nineteenth century, there were records of Chinese settlers in Calcutta (now Kolkata), as it was easy for Chinese people to travel across land and take up jobs as leather workers, a task that Hindus declined for religious reasons. Others trained as carpenters and settled in the Bowbazar area. This low chair with a simple wooden frame looks very contemporary but was actually produced in Calcutta in the early 1900s by Chinese carpenters, using woven cane as the seating material. The height is similar to a Rajasthani *pidda* chair, but has a slight slope extending towards the back.

Aaraam Karna

Carrom board

Date 2013
Designer Precise
Materials Birch plywood,
wood, net

The origins and history of the
game of carrom are unknown
but it is played on a lacquered
piece of plywood, which features
a wooden frame and four net
pockets, one on each corner.
The standard size of the board
is 29 square inches. There
are eighteen pieces (*gottis*)
comprising nine black and nine
unstained wooden discs, and
one red disc called the Queen.
At the start of the game all the
pieces are set in the middle of
the board, with the red Queen
at the very centre. It is ideally
played by two single players,
each assigned either the black
or unstained discs. The aim is to
flick the plastic striker (a larger
piece) against the smaller *gottis*
in order to get their respective
discs, including the Queen, into
the pockets before the opponent
does. Flicking is done with the
thumb and middle finger and
talcum powder is dusted onto
the surface of the board so that
the pieces glide more easily and
with greater precision. Although
not a recognized sport, like
chess, variations of the game
can be found throughout many
countries in Asia, as well as
in parts of Europe.

Yasanche Outdoor Lounge

Date 2013
Designer Yashesh Virkar,
Yasanche and Sandeep Sangaru
Materials Bamboo, rattan

Environmental and
sustainability concerns have
led many designers to explore
and work with bamboo, which
grows rapidly and has a low
environmental impact. A giant
grass with qualities similar
to wood, bamboo grows
abundantly in India, particularly the Katlamara variety,
known for its strength and
durability, which is densely
cultivated around the village
of Katlamara in West Tripura.
Yashesh Virkar's Yasanche
Outdoor Lounge, a hammock-
cum-rocking-chair, is a handcrafted piece of outdoor furniture
that blends traditional craft
with contemporary design. The
curvilinear structure is made
using the bamboo-bending
method, which uses a heating
and cooling technique to flex
it into the desired shape, and
the seating or lounging surface
is woven from rattan. Virkar
(b. 1984), originally from
Mumbai and founder of
Yasanche, worked closely
with designer and manufact-
urer Sandeep Sangaru (b. 1975)
in order to develop his design,
forcing the materials to their
greatest potential.

Pattamadai or Korai mat

Date 2015
Designer Labbai and Rowther communities
Materials Korai grass, cotton

Before furniture was introduced to India, it was the norm to sit on the ground and this is still culturally relevant today, especially in rural Tamil Nadu, for marital and religious rituals. The Labbai and Rowther communites in Pattamadai, Tamil Nadu have long made korai (a member of the sedge, *Cyperaceae*, family of plants) grass *pais* (mats). Softened with the water of the Thamirabarani River, the reeds are split into thread-like strands and handwoven on floor looms by women. The reeds form the warp and fine cotton threads form the weft. Bright colours and geometric patterns from saris (page 252) and dhurrie rugs (page 80) influence the design and the fine reeds also allow for letters, such as the names of a bride and groom, to be woven into these beautiful mats. The finest woven Pattamadai mats, known as *pattu pais*, have a texture that is so silky it is hard to believe they are made of a river grass. Today, natural reed mats, such as this example, are becoming increasingly popular with the urban upper-middle class to reconnect with a certain idea of 'India-ness'.

Hookah or Jajeer

Date 2010
Designer Unknown
Materials Terracotta, bamboo

During the Mughal era, smoking hookah was highly fashionable and is still quite a common practice among people in northern India. A leisurely pastime, smoking a hookah can be done alone or in the company of friends, and has become popular with today's younger generation. Hookah designs and materials keep evolving for a more perfected and hygienic smoke. The basic structure comprises a base filled with water, a hollow shaft, the upper bowl for the coal and tobacco, the smoking pipe and separate metal tongs to stoke the embers. The water bowl can be made in a range of materials such as glass, brass, hollowed coconuts, terracotta, filigree silver and, depending on the region, can feature beautiful decorative details on the base, with florals and geometrics being the most common. The smoking pipe is either straight and fixed or undulates, and can easily be pulled in different directions, making it ideal for sharing and socializing. The terracotta-based hookah, as seen in this example, is commonly smoked by Kashmiri men and is known there as a *jajeer*. It can be seen alongside them during a day's work, ready for a quick puff.

Snakes and ladders

Date 2009
Designer Unknown
Materials Wood

It is said that life is a game of karma, an accumulation of our good or bad deeds, and no other board game better represents this idea than the game of snakes and ladders. The ancient game played by Hindus and Jains was known as *gyaan chapaur* (*gyaan* meaning 'knowledge' and *chapaur* meaning 'square format') or *mokshapath*, which represented the spiritual quest for *moksha* — the release from the cycle of birth and rebirth. It became known as snakes and ladders after its export to England, and as chutes and ladders in the United States. Each player has a token, taking turns to roll the dice and race to the top, moving up with the help of the ladders and back down thanks to the snakes. The snakes may represent the bad deeds that knock your karma back and the ladders an ascending path to salvation. Before the advent of printing on wooden boards and the use of plastic tokens, seen in this modern example, the game would have been painted onto cotton cloth and played with cowrie shells.

Madur

Date 2013
Designer GreenEarth
Materials Madur reed, jute

The connection to the earth remains strong in people's hearts and *madur* or *chatai* (mats, page 168) are essential to this way of life. India has a natural abundance of reeds that can be used for weaving mats, whether they are simple or woven with colours and in ornate geometric designs by local artisans. Just one example of a locally cultivated reed is *madur kathi (Cyperus tegetum)*, which is grown in the swampy area around Midnapore, West Bengal. The quality of the mat depends on how finely the reed has been split. After splitting, the reed is coloured using natural dyes. Bashobi Tewari (b. 1957), graphic designer, established GreenEarth to help village-based craftspeople sell their products. GreenEarth creates three types of reed mat, if the reed weft is handwoven with a cotton warp, it produces a silky *masland* and can be very expensive, whereas a jute warp is used to produce a heavier mat, known as an *ek hara* or *do hara*, as seen here. Such reed mats, which are known to have cooling effects, are eco-friendly and exemplify India's vernacular design culture.

←

Simple stool

Date 2015
Designer Unknown
Materials Wood, laminate

Whether for climbing on to hang clothes to dry, to clean ceiling fans, to fix something in a hard-to-reach spot or simply to rest on at the local *paanwallah*'s (betel-leaf seller), stools like this one are always around. This particular example's design heritage is unknown but was purchased at a market and modified by architect Bijoy Jain of Studio Mumbai Architects. Jain and his team reinforced the stool with strips of recycled wood and added fresh laminate. These simple stools appear regularly on the streets and in homes, be it a modern, upper-class home, or a worker's 3 m² (10 ft²) room. It is a ladder and seating area all in one, and while the *mooda* stool (page 168) or more decorative seats have been recorded and discussed ethnographically, this simple stool is such a key part of the everyday domestic and larger landscape that it can easily be overlooked when considering 'design'.

Kanthas, Rallis and Sujani

Date c. 1970s
Designer Unknown
Materials Cotton

Communities around the country repurpose materials, such as old cotton saris (page 252) and dhotis (page 248), into quilts, using cotton thread in a simple running stitch to join the panels together. These quilts are now coveted around the world, helping to create work for women's self-employment organizations in rural regions. Historical *kanthas* of West Bengal, *sujani* of Bihar and *rallis* made by the nomadic Saami from northwest India and Sindh in Pakistan, are all based on the same principle of layering cloth scraps but have unique regional variations. *Kanthas*, for example, feature either straight running stitch and concentric circles or large elaborate motifs. *Sujani* incorporate storytelling and social narratives into their designs, while Saami *rallis*, as shown here, are known for their black backgrounds with smaller geometric motifs. The dense stitches create a satisfying rippled texture, while the patches used to cover rips and stains add to the graphic feel of the design. These elements, combined with vibrant colours and patterns, make these quilts a joy to own.

Pankhi or Pankha

Date 1950s
Designer Unknown
Materials Brass, cotton silk, metallic thread

Before the introduction of electrical cooling systems, the traditional hand-held fan (*pankhi* or *pankha*) offered reprieve from the heat. These fans, such as this example from the 1950s, are still made and used today, especially when there is a power cut. From simple utilitarian fans made from palmyra leaf, bamboo strips or ramacham roots to ornate fans made from metal or wood with elaborate textile and embroidered decorations, fans are very much part of India's tropical culture and are even used in religious rituals. Local craftsmen, or sometimes women of the household, create the designs, celebrating shapes, techniques and materials that are unique to their region. This example, with its slender brass handle, colourful ruffles and heavy metallic-thread zari embroidery, was most likely owned by a wealthy or royal household.

Charpai

Date 2010
Designer Unknown
Materials Wood, rope

Charpai literally translates as 'four feet', *char* meaning 'four' and *pai* meaning 'feet'. This type of furniture is found throughout villages and urban centres and is present in such a variety of indoor and outdoor spaces that it could easily be overlooked when considering 'design' objects. It is, however, fascinating in its simplicity. It consists of a wooden frame made using mortise and tenon joints (no nails are used) and a series of knotted ropes. Starting at one end, the length of rope is wrapped round the frame and turned back on itself to make an alternating weave that, as well as providing a tensioned elasticity for lying on, creates a beautiful pattern. Traditionally, coir or reused jute rope is used but nowadays strips of recycled plastic packaging, with various metallic colours, abound. The original daybed, the *charpai* is slept on without a mattress or bedding and has been reinterpreted by many contemporary designers. Its origins are obscure yet it features in Indian paintings from the medieval times. It is used for both bringing communities together, by allowing one or more to share the surface to talk or have tea, and for taking a solitary afternoon nap.

←

Bori Sofa

Date 2013
Designer Gunjan Gupta, Wrap
Materials Jute-linen blend, metal frame, foam

A limited edition, with only twenty produced in total, the Bori Sofa comprises a series of parts — made from jute, linen, a metal frame and foam — that can be placed together in various combinations to suit the user. Inspired by the stacks of jute rice bags that tower to unreasonable heights in corner shops and by the workers who sit outside on jute sacks filled with grains and lentils, the Bori Sofa is both humorous and sophisticated. Designer Gunjan Gupta (b. 1974) studied in London before establishing the international design house Wrap in Delhi in 2006, aiming to make Indian product design and handcrafted luxury attractive to an international audience.

Aaraam Karna

खाना-पीना

Khaana Peena

Eating & Drinking

Datta

Date 2015
Designer Unknown
Materials Wood

This ubiquitous little, wooden stamp-like utensil, which measures about 7.5 cm (3 in) in diameter and is around 9 to 10 cm (3¼ to 4 in) high, is used to shape chapattis on a *tawa* (pan, page 222). It is pressed against the chapatti at certain points to allow heat to gather within and creating pockets of air that fluff up the bread. The base of the *datta* is not flat but slightly rounded towards the edges, so that it can be worked from the centre to the outer edges without the dough sticking to it. A variety of materials are used to make *dattas* but wooden ones are favoured as they are less hot to the touch.

Longpi black stone pottery

Date 2013
Designer en Inde, Longpi potters
Materials Serpentine rock, earth

This black pottery has long been made by people of the Tangkhul Naga tribe in the village of Longpi, in Manipur. Locally sourced serpentine rock is crushed and mixed with earth and water to make a clay. The clay is slowly kneaded and then flattened into a wide, long slab, which is rolled out and shaped into a cylinder. Once placed on a circular stand, supported by a stool, the potter moves the cylinder around, holding a stone on the inner side, to hand-mould the desired shape. Cups, pots, plates, bowls and cooking vessels are shaped and left to dry and then fired over an open flame for up to seven hours. They are polished, while still hot, with a local leaf known as the *machee*, which gives the surfaces their greyish-black colour. This type of pottery is often embellished with cane piping around the handles. Anupama Sukh Lalvani (b. 1973) and Sonal Sood (b. 1970), the duo behind en Inde (the Delhi jewellery brand), worked closely with the Longpi potters to create this dinnerware in new designs and devoid of excess decoration. The stoneware has an inherent utilitarian quality — its natural materials retain heat so that food remains hot after cooking.

←

Karhai

Date 2014
Designer Unknown
Materials Cast iron

In the early morning in Chandni Chowk in New Delhi, fresh milk is boiled to the perfect consistency for *mithai*, or milk-based sweets, using a massive *karhai*, or *karahi*. The milk must be watched carefully and stirred slowly, to prevent burning. This cast-iron version from 2014 is one of the larger sizes — *karhais* range from smaller, domestic examples to this industrial size. They are made by blacksmiths in most villages and towns. The *karhai* is often described as being like a wok, having a similar shape and depth, but it is much more heavy duty. It is used for preparing a range of dishes, from deep-fried puris to *jalebis*, and from samosas and *bhaturas* to chicken and beef dishes. These dishes are commonly cooked outside on the streets, tempting passers-by with delicious scents.

Vision Glasses

Date 2015
Designer Borosil Glass Works
Materials Borosilicate glass

The simple, clean lines and contemporary design of the Vision Glass dates back to 1962, when Borosil was established in India in cooperation with Corning Glass Works, USA, who went on to hand over full shares to Borosil in 1988. Borosil produces laboratory glassware and instruments alongside household flameproof kitchenware. The Vision Glasses are made from borosilicate glass (a special soda-lime glass, composed of 75 per cent silica and several additives), which has a resistance to temperatures up to 350 °C/660 °F. The glasses are lightweight, crystal clear and non-porous, with the design most likely based on that of Borosil's laboratory beakers.

Pateelas

Date 2014
Designer Unknown
Materials Stainless steel, copper

The majority of urban kitchens have become modular and Westernized, while rural kitchens are still traditional ones in which preparation and cooking take place on the ground, using fire- or charcoal-based stoves. Utensils and vessels, however, are of the modern era and brass and bell metals have been replaced with affordable and lightweight stainless steel or aluminium. One of the most basic, yet functional, pots used by most households is the *pateela*. A standard cylindrical cooking vessel with a top rim or lip, the *pateela* is used for cooking everything from rice, daals and curries to boiling milk, water and tea, and more. All *pateelas* come with a flat lid and are mostly handleless, so the pot is gripped and lifted using a *pakkad* (page 230).

←

LPG worktop stove

Date 2010s
Designer Unknown
Materials Steel, cast iron, plastic

As *rasoi*, the traditional Indian kitchen, slowly transformed into the Western 'standing-up' style kitchen, so Indian cooking methods changed, too. Before the introduction of LPG (liquid petroleum gas) stoves in the 1970s — which is subsidized and regulated by the Indian government — wood, crop waste, charcoal, dried cow-dung cakes and kerosene were used on *chulhas* (page 202), with each type of fuel imparting its own unique flavour. These traditional fuels are still used, but most urban kitchens use gas stoves and rural areas are increasingly beginning to do the same. This simple stainless-steel worktop gas stove, which can also be built in to the counter, with its characteristic red gas cylinder, is now a common sight in many Indian kitchens.

Ghotni

Date 2015
Designer Unknown
Materials Wood and aluminium

The *ghotni* is commonly made of wood, aluminium or steel and comes in various sizes. The diameter can be quite large, depending on the size of the *matka* (page 214), or pot, it will be used in. This utensil is used for churning buttermilk or lassi. Following Ayurvedic traditions, during the summer months large clay pots of buttermilk (made of yogurt, cumin powder, coriander leaf and rock salt) are kept in the home: the buttermilk is consumed in order to resist disease and to cool the body in order to avoid any possibility of sunstroke. The *ghotni*, such as this example from 2015, is used by holding the stick vertically between both palms of the hands, while plunging the flower-shaped head into the liquid, and rolling the stick between the palms to create a spinning motion. This process helps clear the yogurt of the fat, which rises to the top and can be skimmed off.

Kulfi moulds

Date 2015
Designer Unknown
Materials Aluminium

These simple, lightweight aluminium moulds accompanied by screw-top caps to seal their contents are used to make kulfi — an iconic frozen dessert that is similar to ice cream but much creamier and richer in flavour. Moulds are made out of metal or clay and come in a variety of sizes, sometimes with a wooden stick to be inserted into the frozen dessert as a handle. Kulfi is essentially condensed milk made through a process of laboriously stirring milk over heat, evaporating it to increase the fat content and density, while also caramelizing the lactose and sugar. Once cooled, the liquid is poured into the moulds and tightly sealed. The moulds are then submerged in a clay pot filled with a mixture of ice and salt. The insulating properties of the clay prolong the freezing action, which results in a kulfi that has no ice crystals and is smooth in texture.

←

Kansa tableware

Date 2015
Designer Good Earth, Kansari community
Materials *Kansa*

Kansa is an alloy of copper (85%) and tin (15%). According to Ayurvedic tradition, eating from *kansa* tableware can play an integral role in one's metabolism by importing iron into the body, eliminating free radicals and killing bacteria. The Kansari community in Odisha has been producing *kansa* for centuries, and Indian luxury retailer Good Earth collaborated with them to produce these beautiful bowls. The molten alloy is poured into terracotta moulds (smeared with mustard oil) from which, once slightly cooled, small circular ingots are tapped out. The ingots are then hammered out to create disc-like plates for a variety of utensils. The hammers used for the task come in different sizes, narrow ones are used to spread the ingot quickly, while flatter ones are used to give shape. The disc is continuously heated over a furnace so that it remains malleable enough to be beaten into shape. The finishing process involves grinding, by hand and machine, to even out the edges and polish the interior.

Khaana Peena

Chakki

Date 2009
Designer Unknown
Materials Stone, metal, wood

An essential part of food preparation is the hand-operated *chakki*, a circular stone mortar. Used for grinding rice, wheat and other grains for everyday meals, *chakkis* are used both in the home and in local grinding shops. Two stone discs of equal size are placed one on top of the other, with a central hole in the top disc for pouring in the grains and a metal rod on the base stone to prevent the top stone from sliding off. The base stone remains stationary while the top stone is rotated using a stick handle, producing the grinding action. The pounded grains, or flour, spill out from the gap between the discs and are usually collected by a piece of cloth placed under the *chakki*. Decorative grooves are carved into the surfaces of both stones. Millstones, like the *chakki*, have been traced back to the Paleolithic period.

Chulha

Date Early twenty-first century
Designer Unknown
Materials Mud

This traditional mud stove, although rather antiquated-looking, is still widely used today. It is a true reflection of the lack of efficient basic services in India, such as electricity, which is only available in urban areas and on an irregular basis, making the mud stove the only constantly reliable way of cooking. The stove is made with layers of a mixture of clay and cow dung on a mud base. The front of the stove extends outwards and supports the fuel, which consists of wooden sticks and dung patties (dried cow dung and straw mixed together). Typically, women use the *chulha* and squat in front of it to cook, for instance, rotis on a *tawa* (pan, page 222). This common, simply constructed stove, however, causes a variety of respiratory problems. To combat this, Philips designed a safe low-smoke *chulha* in an attempt to encourage entrepreneurs to produce and distribute them at affordable prices. However, despite winning a number of awards, it has still failed to be widely adopted.

Soop

Date 2010
Designer Unknown
Materials Bamboo, cane

A deceptively simple-looking farming implement, the time-honoured *soop* depends on the forces of nature, gravity and wind to perform its basic function of separating the chaff or husk from grains. The shovel-like *soop* is filled with harvested grains that are then tossed in the air. When done properly, a reasonable wind will blow the lightweight husk away, leaving the heavier grain to fall back into the *soop*. If the air is still, then lighter grains will fall more slowly and land back on top of the pile to be handpicked out. This action will be repeated quickly several times. *Soops* are handmade using bamboo and cane by rural households or by local craftspeople.

Kitchen press

Date 2015
Designer Unknown
Materials Brass

In India, snacks are taken seriously, both in terms of production and consumption. This brass press is used for making *sev, murukku* or *chakli*, variations of fried vermicelli dough that add a crunchy, salty addition to many dishes. While *sev* is made in commercial quantities, smaller batches can also be made at home. The dough is placed in the hollow compartment of the press, of which at the bottom is one of a set of interchangeable discs that are perforated with openings of various sizes and designs, depending on the choice of snack one wants to make. Original kitchen presses comprise two hollow cylinders, one that has holes at the bottom and an internal one that pushes the dough through the holes. The more modern version shown here has a handle at the top that, as it is turned, pushes a plate down against the dough, forcing it through the openings.

←

Chakla and belan

Date 2010
Designer Unknown
Materials Wood

The *chakla* is a raised circular surface, on which leavened dough is rolled to make chapattis or rotis. It is often made from wood or marble but for more ornate versions it is also made from shisham (a kind of rosewood) and includes inlay decoration. The *chakla* has a bevelled edge and a smooth surface, approximately 20 to 23 cm (8 to 9 in) in diameter. The *belan*, or rolling pin, might have handles and a thicker middle section or simply be a long thin stick. Typically these are about 30 to 33 cm (12 to 13 in) long and are usually made from wood, brass, aluminium or granite. The *chakla* is dusted with flour before the dough is placed on it and rolled over in a careful, smooth motion using the *belan*. The *chakla* and *belan* are essential items in a traditional Indian kitchen but are gradually being replaced by roti presses (page 226).

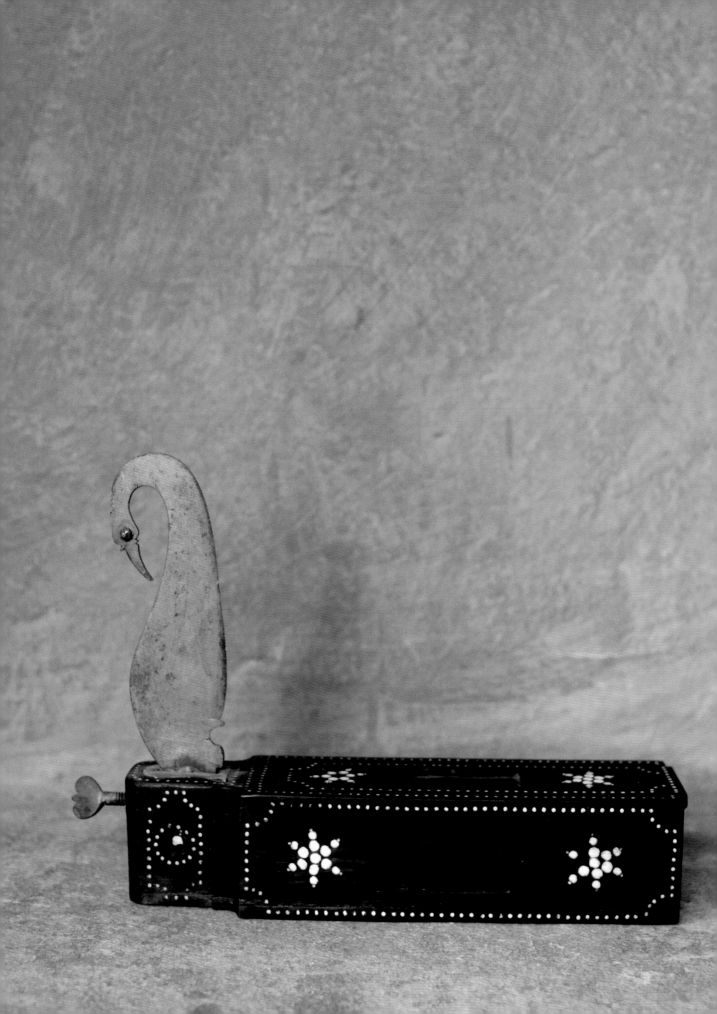

Addoli

Date Early twentieth century
Designer Unknown
Materials Wood, bone, iron

The *addoli* — also known as *bonti* or *hansiya* — is a curved blade, resembling a sickle, that is attached to a wooden platform. This is essentially a stationary knife that is used to chop vegetables and herbs or to grate coconuts. The vegetables are held with both hands and pushed against the blade in a rapid but precise motion. The user squats over the board while chopping and keeps one foot steady on the platform. They are still widely used today, more commonly in the southern states of India, and provide controlled slicing results. This particular example is very decorative, the metal blade resembling a swan or bird and the wooden box with bone inlay. Unlike more rudimentary *addolis*, with plain wooden platforms, this one has compartments for storage, as well as a key for locking up the contents.

Puttu kutti

Date 2015
Designer Unknown
Materials Stainless steel

Puttu, made from ground rice layered with grated coconut and salt or cumin, is a common breakfast dish in Kerala. Water is added to ground rice and then it is layered with coconut and steamed in a *puttu kutti* — a stainless-steel, cylindrical steamer with two sections. The bottom section holds water and the upper section holds the *puttu* mixture. Each section has a perforated lid, allowing steam to pass through. As the *puttu kutti* is placed directly onto the source of heat, it becomes very hot. Newer versions, like this one, are sold with an insulating surface so that it can be held in the middle to pull apart the sections and push the *puttu* out onto a dish. *Puttu*, which means 'portion' in Tamil, can be found throughout Tamil Nadu (served with palm sugar and jaggery — unrefined sugar), Sri Lanka (alongside fish and tripe curries) and Kerala (accompanied by curries, plantain or a sweet black coffee).

Bed-side Carafe and Glass

Date 2012
Designer Rashmi Ranade, Coppre
Materials Copper

Contemporary design studio Coppre, founded by product designer Rashmi Ranade, has been working with metal-working artisans from Tambat Ali — a tiny alleyway in Pune. Tambat (meaning 'coppersmiths' in the Marathi language) were initially brought into the city to produce copper coins, artillery and utensils during the eighteenth century but today only about eighty artisans still have the expertise and continue this craft of hand-shaping and beating copper. Factors such as industrialization and British colonial bans on local production caused the gradual replacement of copper and brass by stainless steel or plastic. Nowadays, INTACH (Indian National Trust for Art and Cultural Heritage) and the Pune engineering company Forbes Marshall, along with Ranade, work together to foster this copper tradition by creating contemporary products that retain Ayurvedic principles, as it is believed that drinking water out of copper can destroy viruses and bacteria, thereby purifying the blood.

Idli stand

Date 2015
Designer Unknown
Materials Stainless steel

Nothing beats a fluffy *idli*, accompanied by *sambar* (a tangy, tamarind-based lentil soup) and coconut chutney all served on a banana leaf. Circular in shape, *idlis* are steamed in an *idli* stand — a set of plates held together by a central rod. The knob unscrews in order to remove each perforated plate and fill the indented moulds with batter. The batter is made by soaking rice and husked *urad dal* (black gram lentils) with fenugreek seeds, grinding the mixture and then leaving overnight to ferment. The stand is placed in a pressure cooker and steamed. There are various kinds of *idli* makers and stands — some in plastic, some electric and some for making mini *idlis*. This modern stainless steel version makes the standard-size *idli*, which is about 7.5 cm (3 in) in diameter. Typically in the south — as it is a southern Indian breakfast — the *idli* is broken into pieces and mixed into the *sambar*. To enjoy the soft texture fully, *idlis* must be absolutely fresh when eaten.

 ←

Coconut scraper

Date 2015
Designer Komal Trading Corporation
Materials Stainless steel, rubber

Coconut flesh is used extensively in Indian cooking, most commonly in South India, where nearly every dish contains either coconut milk or finely grated coconut meat. After cracking the hard outer shell, the inside can be grated or shredded using a variety of kitchen utensils. Traditionally the *addoli* (page 210) is used, but more contemporary versions, such as this worktop scraper, are becoming a common sight. Introduced in the 1980s, they have a rubber base that can be stuck onto a worktop so that sitting or squatting on the floor, as with the *addoli*, is no longer required. Once the coconut is broken in half, the shell is firmly held in place against the circular metal plates, which have tiny teeth. The user then turns the handle to turn the teeth against the flesh and extract the meat. Unlike the *addoli* — a fixed blade against which the coconut is scraped using both hands — here the handle lightens the work.

←

Matka, Handi and Ghara

Date Early 2000s
Designer Unknown
Materials Brass and terracotta

The forms of gourds, melons, mangoes and lotuses inform a multitude of age-old metal and earthen vessel designs to carry and store water and food. The words *ghara* and *matka* are sometimes used interchangeably owing to linguistic variations. Pictured here are two terracotta pots — a *matka* and *handi* — with traces of painted decoration. The unique property of clay pots is their porous surface, which allows heat moisture to evaporate, so creating a cool interior for preserving food and water. *Gharas*, like the hammered brass version here, are specifically used for carrying water. Its distinctive, wide, cylindrical body with a fluted opening allows for the easy collection of water with minimum spillage and a smoother pour. It is an incredible sight to see people carrying *gharas* on their heads to and from their local water source. Once the water arrives at the home, it is usually poured out of the *ghara* into a *matka* to keep it cool and fresh.

Sil batta

Date Early 2000s
Designer Unknown
Materials Granite

Sil — a flat granite, lime or white sand stone — commonly paired with a *batta* — a cylindrical or half-moon shaped stone. Together they create a manual grinder, which is used to make chutneys or to grind fresh spices and masalas. This traditional tool is named after the *silavats*, communities of stonecarvers spread throughout the country. The *sil* has a grooved surface that catches the herbs or spices, which are ground by repeatedly rubbing the *batta* over them. It is used while squatting on the ground in order to utilize upper body strength. The example seen here has the orange stain of turmeric and chilli. Although this heavy, manual grinder has largely been replaced by the electric mixer, it is still found in rural homes and in the homes of those living in cities who cannot afford electrical appliances or do not receive electricity on a regular basis. The taste and texture of some chutneys, like *thecha* from the state of Maharashtra, made from raw garlic, roasted green chilli, peanuts and coriander, cannot be replicated using an electric mixer.

Pressure cooker

Date 2010
Designer United
Materials Steel, rubber, plastic

In the twentieth century, when the pressure cooker was first introduced to India, people were sceptical, yet today it is almost impossible to find an Indian kitchen that does not have one. The pressure cooker eases the workload of producing three fresh meals a day, without sacrificing taste and texture. They are tightly sealed aluminium or stainless-steel pots that cook food in a short period of time under intensely hot steam. Basic elements of the design include a rubber gasket to create an airtight seal, a pressure regulator valve and a safety lock. The pressure cooker has evolved over time and in the late 1930s the first version for domestic use was introduced. In the late 1950s two separate Indian companies — Hawkins and Prestige — collaborated with British companies — L.G. Hawkins and Prestige UK — to manufacture and sell pressure cookers in India. Today, multiple Indian brands manufacture them, including United, which produced this version.

Sumeet Mixer-Grinder

Date Mid-2000s
Designer S.P. Mathur
Materials Stainless steel, plastic

The story goes that Mr S.P. Mathur, an engineer working for German company Siemens, came up with the mechanics of a high-powered motor for a blender that would mix, grind and chop, after his wife's mixer broke down. They agreed that what Indian cooks needed was a robust motor to handle the preparation of ingredients used in Indian dishes. In 1963 the sleek, simple Sumeet Mixer-Grinder, or 'Mixie', was launched and became the middle-class housewife's dream-machine — not only for dry masala mixes, but for the heavy, gloopy batters for *idli* or *dosas*. The platform is long with buttons for turning the motor intensity up by degrees and the container itself is stainless steel — a sturdy, indestructible material. The elegant design seems to celebrate its invention, as the mixer sits high above the motor, conveying a sense of pride.

Chimta and tawa

Date 2015
Designer Unknown
Materials Stainless steel, cast iron

This *tawa* is a cast-iron circular pan. The iconic *tawa* is typically quite flat with slightly upturned edges, although some are entirely convex and some do not have handles so they are lifted using a *pakkad* (page 230). It is used to cook chapatti or roti and to fry small cutlets and fish. Before placing the dough for chapatti onto the *tawa*, the pan must be preheated, otherwise the chapatti will become hard and will crack. The dough is quite soft, as it is made with wheat flour and a fair amount of water, so once it is rolled out it is slapped quickly onto the pan. The chappati is flipped using *chimta* this long, flat, tong-like tool, which was traditionally made in cast iron, but today is manufactured in stainless steel. The *chimta* is an integral part of a kitchen, even in modern kitchens equipped with gas stoves, as it is used to hold a flat-bread or poppadom over an open flame. Unlike a Western pair of tongs, which has a large gripping area at the very end, the *chimta* is flat and thin, suited to holding the edge of the roti so that it can puff up when heated.

←

Kadukas

Date Mid-twentieth century
Designer Unknown
Materials Brass, copper

In India, even the most common *kadukas*, or grater, has an anthropomorphic look, with a head resembling a turtle and four little legs to provide space underneath. *Kadu* means 'pumpkin' and *kas* 'to grate', but the name *kadukas* is rather misleading, as this grater is used for all kinds of vegetables, roots and gourds, not just pumpkin. The 'head' of the grater is used to grate coconut — the coconut can be moved in repetitive motions against the small, sharp grooves to scrape out the coconut meat. This particular example is from the state of Kerala, where one finds coconut in most dishes. It is made in two parts, a copper plate with perforated floral designs and a brass base with legs.

Thali and tumbler

Date 2015
Designer Unknown
Materials Stainless steel

The ubiquitous thali varies across the country — some have twelve *katoris* (small bowls), some have five and some have different-sized plates. It is primarily used for lunch or dinner and the dishes and order in which they are eaten varies throughout the regions and seasons. The thali itself is a high-rimmed plate, which today is mostly made of affordable stainless steel; in earlier times it was made of brass. New designs have compartments or come with a handle that can hold all the *katoris* together, but the classic design is the thali with separate *katoris*. Walking into any *dhaba* or restaurant, one sees thalis, with their *katoris* already positioned on them, stacked high in space-saving columns. There are many varieties of stainless-steel thalis, but this one has a nice, straight, high rim with no extraneous decoration and comes with a matching tumbler for drinking water or buttermilk.

←

Narkel kuruni

Date 2015
Designer Unknown
Materials Metal alloy

Coconut is used in many Indian coastal cuisines and various utensils, including the traditional *narkel kuruni* shown here, are used to extract the flesh from the coconut. Food preparation and cooking still widely take place while sitting on the ground and certain utensils and implements have been designed with this in mind. To use the *narkel kuruni*, one crouches down and places one's foot on the base to hold it in place and scrapes the coconut against the round, serrated head to extract the flesh. A variation of the design features a sharp blade built into the neck that faces towards the person and is used for cutting meat, vegetables and herbs. The advantage of hand-cutting and scraping coconuts is that, unlike a machine, no extraneous heat is produced, which helps to preserve the flavour and texture.

←

Roti press

Date 2015
Designer Classic Enterprise (Industries)
Materials Cast iron, stainless steel

Using a roti press means that, instead of having to roll the dough out using a *belan* (rolling pin, page 206), one simply places it in the roti press, closes the top and squeezes the lever down so that the roti or chapatti is flattened and ready to be placed on the *tawa* (pan, page 222). The exterior is cast iron, making it heavy enough to squash the dough into a flat piece, while the interior is smooth stainless steel. This design was the modern alternative to the rolling pin, but, as always, there are new inventions on the horizon, including a robotic roti-maker called the Rotimatic that automatically mixes flour with water, then cooks and produces freshly made roti.

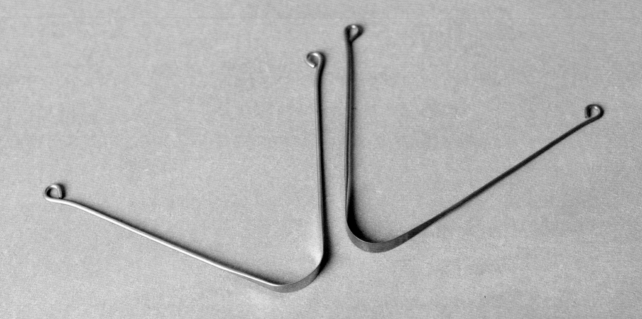

Jeebis

Date 2015
Designer Unknown
Materials Stainless steel and copper

A *jeebi* is used in the mornings to remove toxins, bacteria or dead cells that accumulate on the tongue while we sleep. Using a toothbrush is not considered effective in removing *ama*, or digestive waste, and if these toxins are left on the tongue they are reabsorbed into the body. Ayurvedic traditions regard the tongue as a reflection of, or a window to, the whole body and it will often be looked at first during a medical examination. The Ayurvedic tradition of *jihwa prakshalana* — an oral hygiene practice of scraping the tongue — led to the design of this little innocuous tool, which helps to improve digestion by cleaning taste buds and activating salivary glands. The width of the *jeebi* is about 2 mm (¹⁄₁₆ in), gradually increasing to about 5 mm (¼ in) in the centre curve; this is the section that is used to scrape against the tongue ten to fourteen times, rinsing in between. *Jeebis* are commonly made from copper or stainless steel and are used widely throughout India.

←

Pakkad

Date 2014
Designer Unknown
Materials Steel

The *pakkad*, which means 'to catch or grab', is similar to bolt tongs used by blacksmiths. They come in many sizes and are mostly made in stainless steel or aluminium. The earliest specimens would have been made in cast iron and used with the *pateela* (pot, page 194), which has a protruding lip or edge. The *pakkad* grips perfectly around this lip and could have been designed precisely for this purpose. Made up of two elements held together with one screw, the design enables the user to open and close the utensil and form a firm grip on the *pateela*, which prevents burns and allows for a measured pour. Even today, most cooking vessels do not have handles so the *pakkad* is used to pick them up. This is one of the most used kitchen tools in India and provides greater support for the whole arm, as opposed to holding the handle of a pot and tipping it with the wrist.

Eat Stack

Date 2009
Designer Gunjan Gupta, Wrap
Materials Silver- and gold-plated brass

Designer Gunjan Gupta's desire to bring a contemporary understanding to the vast traditions and visual language that exist in everyday life in India is seen in all of her designs. Her Delhi-based studio, Wrap, has recently transformed the thali (page 226), or common stainless-steel plate, into both an elevated fine-dining set and a stack for decorative and storage purposes. The entire set, made from either silver- and gold-plated brass or solid silver and gold, was initially made for an exhibition at Sotheby's in London. The profile of the stacked thali is instantly reminiscent of temple architecture. When several are stacked around a table it is like seeing a series of structural columns. When disassembled, the set is versatile for both Indian dishes and Western food. Included is a large plate, a smaller plate, a roti plate, two *katoris* (small bowls), a napkin holder and a drinking glass.

पहनना

Pehenna

Wearing

Pashmina shawl

Date 2015
Designer Kashmirloom
Materials Himalayan
goat's wool

Handwoven from the soft
under-wool of the Himalayan
goat (*Capra hircus*), locally
known as the *pashm* goat,
the pashmina shawl is one of
Kashmir's most prized crafts.
Artisans have been hand-
weaving these shawls,
renowned for their softness
and warmth, for centuries.
The looms used to create
them remained unchanged
until the introduction of
mechanized power looms in
the nineteenth century. In
Kashmir, the pashmina shawl
goes through an elaborate
system of processing, weaving
and final cleaning, when it
is beaten and washed along
the banks of the Jhelum River
in Srinagar. Pure 100 per cent
pashmina wool is yarn that is
spun and woven from *pashm*
goat and is not blended with
any other materials. In its
purest form, the pashmina
shawl is undyed (natural
colours range from beige to
brown) and handwoven
without any embellishment
in a simple two/two weft-
faced twill. Contemporary
markets have misrepresented
the pashmina, the word now
commonly referring to any
soft shawl, regardless of
quality and material.

←

Kediya

Date 2014
Designer Unknown
Materials Cotton dyed with
natural indigo

A short, flared jacket with long
sleeves worn by men and boys
of various tribes in areas of
western Gujarat, the *kediya*
is derived from the *angrakha*,
which was introduced during
Mughal times. It features an
overlapping front with long
ties over the chest, underarm
gussets and distinctive pleats
that gather and flare out
below the chest in a skirt-like
fashion. *Kediyas* can be made
in plain white cotton or can be
richly embroidered for special
occasions such as weddings
and festivals. The extra-long
and narrow *churi* (bangle-like)
sleeves are intended to be
ruched up the arm. This *kediya*,
which has been adapted for
mainstream Indian fashion,
has been made for a woman.
It has been dyed using
a natural indigo dye derived
from fermented indigo plants
and features decorative
white thread stitching.

Rakhi bracelets

Date 2015
Designer Unknown
Materials Cotton

Offering and tying a knotted
string represents the creation
of unity, a bond between
two individuals. This simple
innocuous thread, a *rakhi*, offers
protection and derives from the
Sanskrit word *raksh*, meaning
'to guard'. During the traditional
festival of Raksha Bandhan —
held during the Hindu calendar
month of Shravana in August
and celebrated by most Indians
of different religious affiliations
— sisters tie a thread around
the right-hand wrists of their
brothers (both related and
in spirit), seeking protection
and symbolizing the love and
duty they hold to one another.
Threads are traditionally
cotton or silk in a variety of
colours, twisted and topped
with a pompom or rosette-like
decorative element. *Rakhis*
can be handmade or bought so
they are found in many different
varieties, which can also include
red or gold thread, glittery
embellishments, gemstones
and even gold charms.

Gandhi topi

Date 2015
Designer Unknown
Materials Cotton

The Gandhi *topi* (cap) was initially a common man's hat worn by Gujarati men that was adopted by Gandhi in the 1920s as part of his efforts to wear only Indian clothes. It became a symbol of the Swadeshi movement — a nationalist movement for Indian independence from British colonial rule. The adaptation of Indian garments was propagated as a sign of opposition to foreign-made clothes being sold to Indians. The Gandhi cap, similar to the foldable military side cap with a crease, has a hollow centre and is made of thick, *khadi* cotton, which is handspun and handwoven. The cap is still widely worn today in political circles and as part of the uniforms worn by, among others, the famous *dabbawallahs* (tiffin delivery men) of Mumbai.

Nehru jacket

Date 2015
Designer Unknown
Materials Cotton

The Indian gentleman's alternative to a formal blazer or waistcoat, the Nehru jacket is a tailored sleeveless jacket with a band collar and a row of buttons down the front. It looks impeccable when paired with a starched *kurta* (page 244) and pyjama, or worn over a shirt with trousers or dhoti (page 248), and is well suited to the Indian climate. Derived from a shorter waistcoat, known as a *sadri*, the jacket was immortalized by India's first prime minister — Jawaharlal Nehru, who, in the 1940s, adopted the *sadri*, added the band collar (now known as the Nehru collar), and wore one made of *khadi* cotton. *Khadi* cotton was a symbol of India's fight for independence and the Swadeshi movement in opposition to foreign-made clothes. The example seen here was made by the government-run store Khadi Bhandar, found throughout the country and initiated by the Swadeshi movement. Politicians today still proudly wear pure *khadi kurta*, pyjama and Nehru jackets as part of their 'political uniforms', as do fashionable men.

←

Rabari shawl

Date 1950s
Designer Rabari tribe
Materials Sheep's wool, zari

The Rabari are a tribe of pastoralists found in the Kutch region of western Gujarat and are known for their textile and craft traditions, from weaving to hand embroidery. Their shawls are a profound expression of their ancestral craft and cultural identity. Handwoven on looms, using sheep's or goat's wool, the shawls, with their bold colours and patterns against stark bases of dark hues, are visually stunning. Black is a common colour among the Rabaris and various legends are connected to the cultural significance of this colour among the tribe. There are aesthetic variations within the different Rabari clans, but common design factors are the chain stitch, geometric and floral motifs, circular mirror work, embroidered diamond and square patterns and *bandhini* — a tie-dye technique. The colourful elements of the shawls are perfect for cool desert nights and stand out in the bleak desert landscape. Fashion demands have inspired artisans to contemporize some of the shawls, which can be seen worn by urban Indian women throughout the country.

Thaila

Date 2014
Designer Unknown
Materials Nylon

Durable and affordable, brightly coloured nylon *thailas* (bags) with contrasting stripes are part of the modern daily landscape, used for shopping or travelling. They can be used for carrying a variety of items, such as vegetables from the market, and seeing them carried by families travelling by train or bus is a common sight. Nylon and plastic bags are manufactured by many small-scale industrial units throughout India; this is a generic example of the variety of bags they produce. Approximately 51 by 76 cm (20 by 30 in), these box-shaped bags generally cost under 150 rupees (around £2).

Paranda

Date 2015
Designer Unknown
Materials Cotton, metallic thread, rayon

Thick, abundant hair being a sign of beauty for women, the *paranda* is a traditional extension and ornament that both thickens and decorates a plait. Made from cotton, silk, rayon or synthetic yarn, it is separated into three sections, each of which finishes with a tassel. As they are made in various colours, styles and weights, many dancers use the *paranda* to tie and keep their long hair in place. The tassels follow each motion, creating flashes of colour and emphasizing movement. The example shown here is worn by Punjabi women, on special occasions and on their wedding day. Similar plaits called *chotia* or *balchoti* are made in other regions of India by craftsmen that work only with yarn, thread or cord, for both religious and secular purposes.

Kurta

Date 2011
Designer Lal Behari Tandon
Materials Cotton, cotton thread

Made in a variety of lengths (usually below the knees) and girths, the *kurta* features a round neck, a centre-front opening and side slits. The term *kurta* can be traced back to the Turko-Persian tradition, although there is some evidence to suggest that it derives from early Chinese terminology. During the nineteenth century it went from being an undergarment to being assimilated into outerwear and was traditionally worn with a pyjama. Today, *kurta* are made in cottons, silks and various synthetics, both handwoven and mill-made, and range from plain fabrics to embellished ones. The *kurta* shown here features *chikankari* embroidery, a subtle white-on-white shadow embroidery that became popular in Lucknow, Uttar Pradesh during the nineteenth century and still remains fashionable today. It is made of fine cotton and is ideal for hot climates as well as for showcasing the delicate embroidery that is known to have a repertoire of up to thirty-six stitches. *Chikankari* work produced in Lucknow now has GI status (that is, its name is protected by its Geographical Indication tag) and is mostly embroidered by women.

Charkha

Date 1945
Designer Unknown
Materials Wood

A wheel with twenty-four spokes is depicted on the white central strip of the Indian flag, crowned by the saffron strip above and supported by the green strip below. This wheel is part of the historic charkha (spinning wheel, seen here), which became a symbol of India's efforts to gain political independence. In India, it is the ultimate symbol of freedom and emancipation, having been used by Gandhi as part of a revolutionary movement of self-reliance and production to boycott foreign-made cloth. Gandhi's Swadeshi movement, which centred on the production of *khadi* (handspun and handwoven cotton cloth), was created in order to oppose the British policy of purchasing cotton from India at low prices to manufacture clothes in Britain and then sell them to Indian populations. A portable version of the charkha, known as the Yerwada Charkha, was named after the Yerwada Prison in Pune, where Gandhi designed that particular model during his imprisonment there in the mid-1930s.

Katri

Date 2012
Designer Unknown
Materials Scrap metal, steel

A simple tool used by tailors and weavers, the *katri* fits easily into the hand and allows for more controlled cutting or snipping of threads. Local scissor-crafters have a reputation for making scissors and *katri* forged in carbonized steel from scrap metal that are used and well respected by tailors, weavers and barbers. Meerut, Uttar Pradesh, is a major scissor-producing area. Artisans have been making recycled scrap-metal scissors there for generations. This example was being used by pashmina weavers in Kashmir.

Dhoti, Mundu, Veshti

Date 2015
Designer Unknown
Materials Cotton

Elegant and functional, the dhoti is worn by men throughout India. It is a draped lower garment that has existed since Vedic times. It is a single piece of unstitched rectangular cloth, between 2 m (6½ ft) and 4.5 m (14¾ ft) long and 1.25 m (4 ft) wide, that takes the form of a garment once the wearer drapes and folds it around his waist, takes it through his legs and tucks it into his waist at the back. Perfectly suited to Indian climates, the dhoti has many regional variations in terms of draping styles, colours and weaves. White or cream (unbleached) cotton is the most common fabric, followed by silk and synthetics, either hand or mill woven, often with a border in a contrasting colour along the selvedge and end width, such as the thick gold border seen here. Ceremonial or utilitarian, dhotis can be worn with a bare chest or another piece of draped cloth and a *kurta* (page 244) or even a T-shirt. During India's struggle for independence the dhoti became a political symbol, displaying nationalistic pride and self-sufficiency in opposition to the wearing of European-style garments. Dhoti trousers, which have been adopted by the fashion industry for both men and women, are a variation of the traditional dhoti.

Sari

Date 2014
Designer Sanjay Garg,
Raw Mango
Materials Mulberry silk,
metallic thread

If there is one garment that
is synonymous with India, it
is the sari. Tracing its origins
back to ancient India, the sari
is a draped garment worn
throughout India by women of
all ages, classes and religions,
although there are considerable
regional variations in colour,
drape style, motifs and weaves.
Whether worn by elegant
brides in resplendent silks,
construction women in polyester
or politicians in meticulously
starched handloomed cottons,
the beauty of the garment lies
in its functionality. It is a
rectangular stretch of cloth,
made from cotton, silk or
synthetic fabric, ranging in
length and breadth. There
are hundreds of draping styles,
the most popular being the
Nivi, where half the length is
wrapped round the waist while
the other half covers the upper
body and the end part is draped
over one shoulder. Traditionally
handwoven, nowadays the sari
is commonly mass-produced,
although revivalist initiatives
continue the artisan aesthetic.
This stunning example was made
by designer and founder of Raw
Mango, Sanjay Garg (b. 1980),
and is a reinterpretation of the
traditional Benares sari.

Mojari, Mojri, Mojadi

Date 2013
Designer Unknown
Materials Leather, cotton thread

Introduced to India by the
Mughals in the sixteenth century,
the *mojaris* (closely related
to *jutis*), traditionally with
distinctly pointed toes and flat
soles, have evolved into many
styles, with production clusters
throughout the country. *Mochis*
— shoemakers of Jodhpur
(a popular area for making
mojaris) — use soft cow, goat,
camel or buffalo leather for
the uppers and hard leather
for the sole, moulded round
a three-piece wooden cast.
Densely embroidered uppers
in bright colours, made in
threadwork, zari (metallic
thread), wool and leather cut-
outs, are common, although
plain, unembellished leather
shoes are worn by Rajasthani
farmers, for example. The soles
are attached using a thick,
white-cotton chain stitch and
there is generally no distinction
between the left and the right
foot. In general, men carry out
the leatherwork while women
freestyle with the embroidery.
Worn by both men and women,
mojaris have become extremely
popular in recent years,
especially for weddings
and occasion wear.

Khadi towels

Date 2015
Designer Khadi and Village Industries Commission
Materials Cotton

Made from handspun cotton, handwoven cotton towels are lightweight and appropriate for the Indian climate, as they are absorbent and fast-drying. A contrasting border along the selvedge(s) and sometimes across the centre is a common design feature, also found in other Indian textiles, such as *gamchas* (opposite), dhotis (page 248) and saris (page 252). The term *khadi* is derived from *khaddar*, which means a handspun and handwoven cotton cloth that becomes softer and suppler with use. The Khadi and Village Industries Commission, or KVIC, established in 1956 is known for making and selling all types of affordable *khadi* clothes and textiles, such as the towels seen here.

←

Gamcha

Date 2015
Designer Unknown
Materials Cotton

A coarse cotton cloth thrown over the shoulders of men, or around their necks, is a common sight throughout India. Simple and utilitarian, the iconic *gamcha* is used as a towel for drying after bathing or for wiping away sweat, for wrapping the head to protect it from the sun, as padding when balancing items on the head, or simply as a scarf. Both handwoven and mill-made *gamchas* come in a range of colours from blues to greens and whites, but red is the most common and all feature woven checked and striped patterns. They are normally associated with labourers and rural men, but have become fashionable as an accessory worn by urban men in recent years.

Salwar or Shalwar

Date 2014
Designer Unknown
Materials Cotton

A garment based on the Persian *pyjama*, meaning 'leg covering', the *salwar* is worn by men and women of all backgrounds, religions and ages. There are several variations of the *salwar*, using lengths of fabric ranging from 2 to 5.5 m (6½ to 18 ft) and a varying number of pleats that stitch into the *izaarband* (drawstring waist) — the *patiala salwar* being the most voluminous. The hem also varies in width and length and can be embroidered in the same colour as the fabric. *Salwar* are traditionally made from lightweight fabrics such as cotton, silk or synthetics and are especially comfortable to wear in the extreme heat. With the *salwar*, women often wear a matching *kurta* (page 244) or *kameez* (a tunic-like top) and a *dupatta* or *odhani* (a veil-like wrap), which as an ensemble is called a *salwar kameez*.

Naga shawl

Date 2014
Designer Chakhesang tribe
Materials Wool and acrylic

Nagaland, a state in Northeast India, is inhabited by sixteen major tribes who contribute greatly to the incredible design diversity and history that exists within India as a whole. Each tribe has its own unique set of textiles that exemplify a visual design language centred around social structure, status and honour. The textiles are predominantly handwoven by women on very simple handlooms, which are partially belted around the weavers' bodies. The design patterns and sizes are therefore restricted, resulting often in a cotton or woollen textile that is woven in three separate panels and stitched together after weaving. The textiles are characterized by distinctive colour combinations of reds, dark blues, blacks, whites and hints of yellow in bold stripes, which are combined with geometric patterns such as zigzags, squares and lozenges. Some pieces are also embellished with cowries and woollen fringes. Until recently, colours were obtained from natural dyestuffs but nowadays these are gradually being replaced by chemical substitutes as well as commercially available cloths.

Bihar Sari Dress

Date 2013
Designer Rashmi Varma
Materials Cotton

The beauty and grace of the sari (page 252) could never be superseded, but they are starting points for the Bihar sari dress. A hybrid of the sari, that is stitched to a constructed bodice, the dress can be worn any time and provides the feel and elegance of the draped sari. It is made in a fine handwoven cotton from West Bengal. The area is historically famed for its cottons or *muls*, which, during the Mughal era had poetic names such as *abrawan* (running water) or *shabnam* (morning dew). The delicate hand embroidery running along the seams is *chikankari*, which is a traditional white on white shadow embroidery from Lucknow, Uttar Pradesh. The word *Bihar* refers to the turmeric-yellow colour commonly used in the state of Bihar for religious- and wedding-related garments. This sari dress was designed in 2013 by Rashmi Varma and is part of a permanent collection at the Victoria and Albert Museum in London.

रखना

Rakhna

Holding

Fela Clutch

Date 2012
Designer Mia Morikawa and Shani Himanshu, 11.11 / eleven eleven
Materials Reclaimed plastic bags, organic *kala* cotton threads, metal

The work of Khamir, an NGO and platform for craft revival in the Kutch district of Gujarat, and ethical fashion label 11.11 / eleven eleven, the handmade Fela Clutch addresses the issue of plastic waste, conspicuous consumption and the desire to transform discarded materials into new and innovative products. Plastic grocery bags — which are often burned in large piles — are collected, cleaned, sorted and cut. The strips are handwoven on a loom, the weft being set with the reclaimed plastic and the warp being made of *kala* cotton. This type of cotton is a rare species that naturally grows in arid regions such as Kutch, thus requiring very little irrigation, and is cultivated organically, without using any fertilizers. The combination of organic cotton and recycled plastic offers a creative solution for mitigating environmental problems and encouraging craft livelihoods.

←

Asana (Warrior Pose) table

Date 2012
Designer Farzin Adenwalla, Bombay Atelier
Materials Steel, glass

Defining a certain modern Indian aesthetic while using traditional techniques and working with local craftsmen is the ethic of design company Bombay Atelier, set up in Mumbai in 2008 by Farzin Adenwalla. Originally from New Zealand but of Parsi descent, Adenwalla uses and refers to everyday busy cities like Mumbai in her minimalist designs. The Asana is made with black lacquered glass and a frame of mild steel that balances the materials. Referring directly to the influence of yoga in the West, this table is a conversation between Indian-made craftsmanship and what is popularly considered as Western modernism. Like the yoga Warrior Pose — or the *Virabhadrasana* — the legs of this table bend and stretch in contrasting directions while the glass on top signifies the centring core of the position.

←

Bhadak

Date 2014–2015
Designer *Kumhars* Ibrahim Isa Ali and Adbul Hussain
Materials Terracotta, rope

The traditional *bhadak* has been used for centuries and was made by potters to carry water on the back of a camel in the arid desert region of Kutch in western Gujarat. Ropes made by weaving dried leaves were wound around the *bhadak* to make it easier to carry, as well as to prevent breakage. The *bhadak*, like most pottery in India, is made by men, while the preparation of clay and any decoration is done by women. The various forms and shapes were made keeping in mind utility, function and the customs and aesthetics of the region and users alike. This piece was part of the Ghadai project, a collaboration between Khamir, a native NGO, and the international luxury brand Hermès, which brought together Kutch *kumhars* (potters) to create new pieces for exhibiting in their store in Mumbai. *Ghadai* refers to the technique of pottery employed in the Kutch region and the project facilitated the research and revival of these traditional techniques. This *bhadak* reinterprets an ancient form into a larger-than-life size, with the rope produced in red.

Conch-shell box

Date Early twentieth century
Designer Unknown
Materials Wood

In the *Mahabharata*, at the beginning of the great battle between the Kauravas and the Pandavas, Krishna is said to have sounded his *sankha*, or conch shell, known as Panchjanya. The conch shell, found in the Indian Ocean, has been used through the ages as a trumpet to gather people and to produce a low humming sound during Hindu prayers. Its sound is also used during ritual purification, it is one of the auspicious symbols in both Jainism and Buddhism and the shell itself is used in Ayurvedic treatments. The early twentieth-century storage box shown here is of vermilion-painted wood. The interior is incised with the spiral shape of the conch shell and overall mimics the shape of the *yoni* or womb.

←

Masala dabba

Date 2015
Designer Unknown
Materials Stainless steel

For Indian dishes, a cook needs to have several spices ready to hand. The masala (spice) *dabba* (container) is the perfect design solution. In the past, these would have been made of wood, with a sliding lid. Today, the modern *dabba* is made from stainless steel and has seven inner containers for various spices. The spices it contains depend on the part of the country. Typically, the containers hold turmeric (*haldi*); cumin (*jeera*) — both ground and in seed form; ground coriander seeds (*dhania*); red chilli powder (*mirchi*), and mustard seeds (*sarson*). The *dabba* comes with a tiny spoon and has an airtight cover to keep the spices fresh and dry.

Spiro

Date 2015
Designer Thukral and Tagra
Materials Terracotta

The Spiro terracotta speaker dock explores the idea of combining sustainable handcrafts and evolving technology. Designed by the artist duo Thukral and Tagra (Jiten Thukral, b. 1976 and Sumir Tagra, b. 1979), Spiro is a tongue-in-cheek creation based on their own environment: the cyber-city hub of Gurgaon that adjoins New Delhi and is a techno city that has evolved in the midst of surrounding agricultural land and villages. Thukral and Tagra worked with traditional hand potters of the region to make this two-part speaker dock in which a wireless speaker fits onto a round base and is encased by a cylindrical dome-headed cover. Cut-outs in the cover allow the sound — which travels up from the base — to be transmitted. Spiro is a playful reflection on the times in which we live.

Bharani

Date 2015
Designer E.I.D-Parry
Materials Stoneware

Bharani (also known as *jaadi* in South India) are heavy, non-porous, stoneware containers produced in a variety of sizes, ranging from cylindrical shapes to smaller, rounded pots. They were originally produced by E.I.D-Parry, a British company established in Chennai, who made the iconic, glazed, two-tone brown-and-white jars for the import and transport of chemicals in the 1900s. Once used, they were sold to the public for reuse and their size and sturdiness lead to their adoption as the perfect containers for making and storing pickles. The brown-and-white containers are a common sight on rooftops, where they stand baking in the sun, vermilion-stained oil dripping from their lids. This mustard-infused oil is included in the preparation of *achar* (mango pickle), which is made, cured and stored in large batches for shared households. Today the *bharani* are manufactured by Bajrang Ceramic Industries in Thangadh, Gujarat, an important centre for ceramic production, including sanitary ware and tiles.

Jhadu

Date 2015
Designer Unknown
Materials Grass, plastic

The *jhadu*, such as this example from 2015, is an inexpensive broom that is popularly used throughout the country. It is made from 1 to 1.5 m (3 to 5 ft) of dried grass and twigs, which are tightly bundled together and bent, creating a stub that is then wrapped with a metal or plastic casing and used as a handle. It is affordable and, owing to the prevalence of dust in Indian environments, is one of the most essential domestic items around. They are used by domestic staff commonly hired by many households across the country to clean the home on a daily basis. Government-employed road cleaners use a much thicker and stiffer version for thorough cleaning on cement or brick-paved streets and on both wet and dry surfaces. Newer versions are made in plastics and rubbers, adding to the variety of this economical and eco-friendly everyday item.

Bhel Puri side table

Date 2013
Designer Sian Pascale, Young Citizens
Materials Burma teak hardwood, powder-coated steel

Claimed to be Mumbai's first boutique hotel, Abode's interior was designed by Sian Pascale, an Australian designer who lived in India for a few years. During her time in India, Pascale combed the streets and pulled out some of the most 'unnoticed' objects of everyday life, on which to base her designs. This side table was directly inspired by the ingenuity of the handmade bhel puri stand (page 142) street hawkers use to make and sell bhel puri, a puffed-rice snack. The tables were designed for the hotel and are made from recycled Burma teak hardwood, with a large, black, powder-coated thali plate (page 226) that is not fixed to the base — similar to the construction of the stand. The tables, too, are all handmade and, in this way, the hotel and the furniture within reflect the character of the city outside. Abode takes aspects from the busy street life and local architecture around the areas of Fort and Colaba in south Mumbai and moves them forward into the contemporary.

Betel-leaf tray and lime box

Date Twentieth century
Designer Unknown
Materials Brass

The use of *tambula* — comprised of betel nut, *chuna* (slaked lime, or calcium hydroxide, mixed with water) and a variety of spices, nuts and fruits rolled in a betel leaf — is a tradition that dates back many centuries. While it was introduced by Southeast Asia, Hindus place great social significance on chewing what is now called *paan* (from the Sanskrit word *parna*). Exchanging *tambula*, or *paan*, was connected to sealing the terms of a marriage between families, to worship of the deities and to visits, when a host would offer it to a guest. This brass tray, from the mid-twentieth century, is cast in one piece, with two peacocks incised into the centre. Its shape perfectly frames the form of the betel leaf. It was made in Moradabad, Uttar Pradesh, which is historically known for brassware made by Muslim craftsmen who settled there during the Mughal period. This early-twentieth-century brass betel lime box is from neighbouring state, Rajasthan. Its shape takes inspiration from the mango. The box opens on its hinges to reveal the attached spatula used for making and spreading the *chuna*.

Damchiya

Date Late twentieth century
Designer Unknown
Materials Wood, mirror

Traditional *damchiyas*, or dowry chests, from the western regions of Rajasthan and Gujarat have become popular collector's items both in India and abroad and are used as side tables, consoles and minibars. They are still made for their original purpose, in anticipation of a girl's marriage, as a place for her to keep special items such as textiles and jewellery, which she will take into married life. Handcarved, shallow woodwork in relief and inlay mirror work reflect age-old traditions of woodwork in western India — a region of many nomadic peoples with influences from, and connections to, Central Asia, Iran, Pakistan and Afghanistan. The outside of the hardwood chest, with its cupboard-like doors, is carved with geometric designs of squares, medallions, triangles, florals, sunbursts and quatrefoils, which are also seen in architecture, textiles and other objects from the regions.

←

Rehal

Date c. 1920s
Designer Unknown
Materials Wood

This is a classic version of a foldable bookrest for holy scriptures, used by Hindus, Sikhs and Muslims. The two moving elements are carved from one piece of wood and the folding mechanism has no external hinges. Because praying is done while seated on the ground, the stand is also placed on the ground and opens to the perfect angle at which to keep a book open. The carved, painted, wooden stand seen here is in the incredibly beautiful Jalali House in Srinagar, a 152-year-old house that belongs to descendants of a family who fled persecution in Iran. *Rehals* are still produced today and more modern versions are made from plastic.

Tokri

Date 2015
Designer Unknown
Materials Bamboo, rattan

All along Tulsi Pipe Road, which runs along the Western Line of the Mumbai Suburban Railway, are trucks by the roadside selling vegetables and flowers. The vegetables are displayed in *tokri*, or baskets, which are made on the spot. Mostly bamboo and rattan are used, split into the required widths and the pieces woven together, radiating outwards from the base. There are many varieties of this historic basket, depending on the region and what is carried in them. Baskets made in the plains are typically wider and shallow, while those from the northeast are deep and narrow.

Mug and balti

Date 2015
Designer Unknown
Materials Plastic

The uses for this humble icon of Indian lifestyle, now made of plastic in a variety of colours but originally of steel or brass, vary from washing clothes to bathing. In some cases, water is only available at specific times of the day, so the *balti* (bucket) is also used for storing water. In the past, hot water was boiled in large amounts, added to the *balti* and then cooled by adding cold water. The water would then be poured over oneself using the mug. The *balti*, which holds about 20 litres (5 gallons) of water, provides the perfect amount for a complete bath, conserving water that is otherwise wasted from an overhead shower nozzle. Shower fixtures are relatively new in India and the classic mug and *balti* is seen absolutely everywhere — from low-income housing to new, modern apartments. Whether or not a bathroom has the latest line in fittings, it will often have a shy *balti* sitting in the corner, too.

←

Kophi basket

Date Late twentieth century
Designer Khonoma village craftsmen
Materials Cane

The elegant form of the *kophi* basket, with its unique geometric proportions, is quite feminine and so it seems natural that it should be a symbol of the Angami Naga man's commitment to marry his future bride. Its quality also represents the groom's social status. Highly skilled craftsmen in the village of Khonoma, Nagaland, are responsible for creating these traditional intricate baskets, which are handwoven over a bamboo mould, using evenly cut strips of cane (preferred to bamboo as it is more durable). The square base of the basket rises vertically and flares out towards the top, like the bell of a trumpet, into a circular rim. There is an attached head strap that is partially plaited and woven, which is placed on the forehead and the basket rested on the upper back. The basket can be used for carrying and storing everyday items, such as vegetables and fish, and is supported by dainty feet made of bamboo nodes.

Terracotta bowl

Date 2014
Designer Manjari Nirula and Om Prakash Galav
Materials Red clay

The simple and elegant design of this terracotta bowl, commissioned by the Crafts Council of India and made by potter Om Prakash Galav (b. 1983) of Ramgarh Clay Pottery, hints at a harmonious cross-cultural exchange that has existed between India and Japan since the seventh century AD, when Buddhism was first introduced to Japan. The Crafts Council of India was founded in 1964 by Kamaladevi Chattopadhyay and works with artisans to promote fine craftsmanship and innovation. Manjari Nirula, a volunteer from the council, worked with Om Prakash in 2014 to design a set of terracotta bowls, inspired by Japanese rice and tea bowls. In pure red clay without the use of any lead or paint, they are made in a craft-rich region of Alwar, Rajasthan, where hundreds of potters practise their craft. Indo-Japanese sensibilities of purity, simplicity and hand-created textures along with craft traditions such as pottery, indigo dying, textile weaving and *shibori* or *bandhini* (tie-dye) have inspired many creative collaborations between Indian and Japanese artists and designers.

←

Bowl Table

Date 2011
Designer Ayush Kasliwal
Materials Mango wood, cast iron

The Bowl Table, designed by Ayush Kasliwal, is an elegant mango-wood table with powder-coated cast-iron legs. Its design was inspired by the traditional kneading bowls used by the Chettiar community in Tamil Nadu for kneading roti and other flatbread dough. The Chettiars, a merchant caste that often traded in Myanmar (Burma), adopted the Burmese bowls, typically made from single pieces of teak lacquered with bright-orange shellac. The Bowl Table comes in three sizes and is easily dismantled so that the table can be used by itself as a wooden tray or for transport purposes.

Bidri business-card box

Date 2014
Designer Unknown
Materials Zinc and copper alloy, Bidar soil, silver inlay

Metals from the earth and the unique properties of soil are instrumental in producing *bidri ka kaam*, or bidriware, an age-old technique practised predominantly in Bidar, Karnataka. Bidri objects are handcast using an alloy of zinc and copper, which gives them their distinctive part-lustrous and part-matt-black surface. Once the object is formed, a metal stylus is used to etch the design, which is then inlaid with silver or brass. The black surface is sanded down and removed, ready for the final step in the process. A special variety of soil found only in Bidar is mixed with an ammonium chloride paste, which permanently blackens the surface but not the inlay. It is not known why the soil mixture forces the metal alloy surface to oxidize and blacken. This business-card box is just one example of the variety of contemporary objects made using the ancient bidri technique, others include vases, ashtrays, plates and jewellery.

Ayasa Storage Containers and Milk Pourer

Date 2014
Designer Tiipoi
Materials Copper, tin, neem wood

The Ayasa Milk Pourer has an extended 90-degree rim on one side, making it drip-free. This design element takes inspiration from everyday items traditionally found in the Indian kitchen, particularly the *pateela* (pot, page 194), which has this lip on all sides, allowing for a perfect, measured pour. Made in copper or brass and lined with tin, the milk pourer is made in Bangalore by metal spinners who take a disc of metal and rotate it at a high speed either by hand or machine. The storage containers, made in the same way, are stackable with neem wood lids. Tiipoi, founded in 2013 by Spandana Gopal, is a London-based lifestyle brand that works with various manufacturing set-ups in India and aims to meld the hand- and machine-made. They are interested in appropriating and highlighting existing design features found in everyday utensils and reintroducing the use of copper over cheaper, imported plastics.

Godrej Almirah

Date c. 1970s
Designer Godrej
Materials Steel

Before the year 2000, when credit cards were introduced into the wider economy, buying a house or car in India meant paying the full price, upfront, in cash. Therefore, storing money and valuables securely was of great concern, which is where the story of the Godrej Almirah begins. The founder of Godrej — Ardeshir Godrej — was a lawyer who wanted to create products within India that could really compete against foreign brands. He began to manufacture locks in 1897 and developed the very first Indian safe in 1902, which then evolved to being fitted inside a stand-alone metal wardrobe. This wardrobe, known as the Godrej Almirah, was expensive and a symbol of the upper-middle class, replacing the traditional wooden wardrobes. Inside was the prized safe plus enough room for storing saris and suits. The outer door also had a lock so one could truly feel one's possessions were secure in the home, even with the coming and going of servants, and the jangle of keys heard emanating from the sari of the householder became a familiar sound. This wardrobe is not the most attractive nor most sophisticated design but it is an icon and is integral to the household.

←

Mister Chai

Date 2013
Designer Farzin Adenwalla, Bombay Atelier
Materials Teak wood, polyurethane, stainless steel

When one looks at the base of this teak-wood-topped table and sees the scalloped edges of the frame, the name Mister Chai becomes clear. The base of the table resembles the iconic chai glasses (page 102) that are used on every street corner to serve tea. Farzin Adenwalla, a young designer from New Zealand, established Bombay Atelier in Mumbai, taking direct cues from the busy, bustling environment around her. She understood that good design already existed and would need little change and so the up-turned chai glass becomes the base of this coffee table, made from stainless steel. It is a brilliant example of incorporating everyday street culture into contemporary design.

Lota

Date Nineteenth century
Designer Unknown
Materials Brass

Tipping water into the mouth without touching the rim of the drinking vessel is a traditional way of drinking water without contaminating the vessel. The *lota* – meaning 'vessel' – has an open, flower-like spout that allows one to hold the vessel in the narrow part of the neck and tip it for a perfect direct pour. This ancient vessel, which references nature in its simple, gourd-like shape is multipurpose; it is used for drinking, washing and ritual, being one of the eight articles required for prayer by Hindus, and also holds blessed water or *gangajal* (water from the Ganges). The *lota* is made in various areas across the country. All owners clean their brassware daily with a mixture of ash and tamarind, for hygiene purposes. Because the *lotas* are polished daily, there is no raised ornamentation, only engraving. This *lota* is from Kutch, Gujarat, and is made from brass, with floral engraving and an overall net-like patterning.

WaterWheel

Date 2015
Designer Wello
Materials Polyethylene plastic, powder-coated steel

A socially innovative design, the WaterWheel was created in 2015 by non-profit organization Wello to ease the burden of daily water collection in rural regions. Women collect water from wells for their household's daily needs and carry it back in heavy containers on their heads. These wells can be several kilometres from their homes and the task is time-consuming and can lead to severe pain and spine damage. The WaterWheel is an affordable and ergonomic solution that enables the collection and transportation of up to five times more water – as much as 45 litres (10 gallons). The body of the wheel is made of high-density polyethylene plastic and the handle is made of powder-coated steel, making it durable and easy to handle on all types of terrain. The shape of the WaterWheel was derived from traditional water carriers, such as terracotta *gharas* and *matkas* (page 214). The familiar shape maintains cultural relevance but comes with handles on either side to allow for easier pouring and filling.

Dish rack and utensils

Date 2015
Designer Unknown
Materials Stainless steel

Until the 1950s, when stainless steel was introduced into domestic life, nearly all kitchenware was either earthenware, brass – lined with tin – or copper. Corrosion-resistant stainless steel is ideal for the wall-mounted dish rack as it is where washed utensils are put up to dry. This is a domestic rack, which has survived the introduction of modern kitchens with built-in storage; it varies in size and price but is affordable and accessible for all. From bottom left to right are: the *jharo*, which is used for frying, with holes in the bowl section for draining oil. Above it is a tiny ladle, the *karchi*, with a curved handle that rests on the finger while scooping out lentils. Next is the rice spoon, which has a long, angular bowl that enables serving of freshly steamed rice without breaking it up. Below it is the *palta*, a flat-headed tool for sliding under fish as it cooks on a *tawa* (pan, page 222). To the right are serving spoons. Then there is the ubiquitous tea strainer, found in stainless steel in the home and in plastic on the street. It is used to catch tea leaves and other ingredients when making masala chai. Above the classic utensils are thalis (plates, page 226), tumblers, *katoris* (small bowls) and *matka* (page 214).

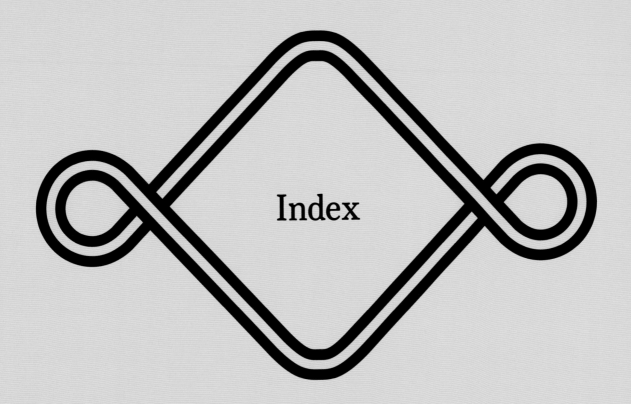

Index

Bibliography

George C.M. Birdwood, *The Industrial Arts of India* (London, 1884)

Robert F. Bussabarger and Betty Dashew Robins, *The Everyday Art of India* (New York, 1968)

Rta Kapur Chishti, *Saris of India: Tradition and Beyond* (New Delhi, 2010)

Steven Cohen, Rosemary Crill, Monique Lévi-Strauss and Jeffrey B. Spurr, *Kashmir Shawls: The Tapi Collection* (Mumbai, 2012)

Ananda Kentish Coomaraswamy, *The Arts & Crafts of India & Ceylon* (London & Edinburgh, 1913)

Ilay Cooper, John Gillow and Barry Dawson, *Arts and Crafts of India* (London, 1996)

Jasleen Dhamija, *Indian Folk Arts and Crafts* (New Delhi, 1970)

Jasleen Dhamija and Jyotindra Jain, *Handwoven Fabrics of India* (Ahmedabad, 1989)

Arindam Dutta, *The Bureaucracy of Beauty: Design in the Age of its Global Reproducibility* (New York, 2007)

Eiluned Edwards, *Textiles and Dress of Gujarat* (Ahmedabad, 2011)

Judy Frater, *Threads of Identity: Embroidery and Adornment of the Nomadic Rabaris* (Ahmedabad, 1995)

Annapurna Garimella and John Xaviers, *Vernacular, in the Contemporary: Part 1 and Part 2* (New Delhi, 2010 & 2011)

Brijinder Nath Goswamy, Kalyan Krishna and Tarla P. Dundh, 'Indian Costumes in the Collection of the Calico Museum of Textiles: 18th to mid-20th Century mostly from North and Western India', Historic Textiles of India at the Calico Museum, vol. V (Ahmedabad, 1992)

Percival Griffiths, *The History of the Indian Tea Industry* (London, 1967)

Thomas Holbein Hendley, *Indian Jewellery* (London, 1909)

Ranjit Hoskote and Ilija Trojanow, *Confluences: Forgotten Histories from East and West* (Delhi, 2009)

Amin Jaffer, *Luxury Goods from India: The Art of the Indian Cabinet-maker* (London, 2002)

Jyotindra Jain, *Utensils: An Introduction to the Utensils Museums Ahmedabad* (Ahmedabad, 1984)

Jyotindra Jain and Aarti Agarwal, *Museums of India: National Handicrafts and Handlooms Museum, New Delhi* (Ahmedabad, 1989)

Jutta Jain-Neubauer, *Feet & Footwear in Indian Culture* (Ahmedabad, 2000)

Jaya Jaitly, *The Craft Traditions of India* (New Delhi, 1990)

Shanay Jhaveri, ed, *Western Art and India: Creative Inspirations in Art and Design* (London, 2013)

Stella Kramrisch, *Unknown India: Ritual Art in Tribe and Village* (Philadelphia, 1968)

Abigail McGowan, *Crafting the Nation in Colonial India* (New York, 2009)

Asharani Mathur, *Indian Shawls: Mantles of Splendour* (New Delhi, 2004)

Sumati Morarjee, *Tambula: Tradition and Art* (Bombay, 1974)

Aditi Ranjan and M.P. Ranjan, *Handmade in India: Crafts of India* (Ahmedabad, 2009)

M.P. Ranjan, Nilam Iyer and Ghanshyam Pandya, *Bamboo and Cane Crafts of Northeast India* (New Delhi, 1986)

Ardhendusekhar Ray, *Crafts and Technology in Ancient India (From the Earliest Times to the Gupta Period)* (New Delhi, 1998)

Archana Shah, *Shifting Sands; Kutch: A Land in Transition* (Ahmedabad, 2013)

Durgesh Shankar, *Crafts Of India And Cottage Industries* (New Delhi, 2003)

Sushama Swarup, *Costumes and Textiles of Awadh: From the Era of Nawabs to Modern Times* (New Delhi, 2012)

Andrew Topsfield, *The Art of Play: Board and Card Games of India* (Mumbai, 2006)

Oppi Untracht, *Traditional Jewelry of India* (London, 1997)

Kumar H Vyas, *Design: The Indian Context: Learning the Historical Rationale of the Indian Design Idiom* (Ahmedabad, 2000)

www.khamir.org

www.gaatha.com

Acknowledgements

We would like to thank the many curators, artists, designers, historians and artisans who showed us techniques and their working environments. A special thanks goes to M.P. Ranjan, Jyotindra Jain and Divia Patel, for various discussions about the past, present and future of design. We are grateful to the following people for advising us, lending items from their personal collections and inviting us into their private spaces for research and photography: in **Ahmedabad** and **Kutch** — Tanisha Kachru, Meera Goradia / KHAMIR, Mr. Surendra Patel / Vechaar Museum of Utensils, Calico Museum of Textiles, Lohar Haji Siddiq, Abdul Jabbar Khatri, Shamjibhai Vankar, Vadha Bhaiya Bhachaya, Dr. Ismail Mohamed Khatri, Sufiyan Khatri, Kinnari Lakhia, Aparajita Basu and Anand Patel, Abhay Mangaldas / House of MG, Wahidbhai; in **Jaipur** — Ayush and Geetanjali Kasliwal, Indu Singh / Meghniwas, Rachel Bracken-Singh / Anokhi Museum, Lassiwala, Max Modesti, Jaipur Modern, Amrapali Jewelers, Priti at Neemrana Village; in **Delhi** — Anita, Anupam Poddar / Devi Art Foundation, Aditya Srinivas, Kuldeep Kaur / Serendipity, Sanjay Garg / Raw Mango, Gunjan Gupta / WRAP, Abheet Gidwani, Nira Kehar, Crafts Museum, Jyotindra Jain, Mrinmoy Das, Museum of Everyday Art / Sanskriti Foundation, Sonal Sood & Anupama Sukh Lalvani / en Inde, Anumitra Ghosh / Big Bong Theory, Thukral & Tagra, Kriti Sachdev, Pramod Kumar / Eka Cultural Resources, Aman Khanna, Qiyuum Masterji, Achinto, Obais Masterji, Ricky Kher / Kardo, Kanika Pruthi, Kamala Craft Shop, Sahil & Sarthak, Sanjivani & Abhimanyu Singh, Mrs. Uma Anand, Dr. Alka Pande, Gitanjali Kolonade, Laura Quinn; in **Srinagar** — Princess Jyotsna Singh / Almond Vilas, Mr. Shabir, Mr. Vakil / Vakil Manzil, Kashmirloom, Samina Zaidi, Syed Iftikhar Hussain Jalali / Jalali Heritage House, Behram; in **Mumbai** — Abode Bombay, Rooshad Shroff, Neerja Shah, Mehma Tibb, Divya Thakur / IndiaUrban, Bijoy Jain / Studio Mumbai Architects, Naheed Carrimjee, Hermès, Beenu Bawa, Good Earth, President — Vivanta by Taj, Suri Gopalan, Manjiri Rajopadhye, Matthieu Foss, Babbu, Farzin Adenwalla / Bombay Atelier, Akansha Nanda, Savio Jon, Cynthia Koenig & Shradha Rao / Wello, Tarini Jindal, Ankur Tewari; in **Patna** — Yashendra Prasad; in **Bhubaneswar** — Kanchan Charan; in **Bangalore** — Malika V Kashyap, Spandana Gopal / Tiipoi; in **Chennai** — Manasa Prithvi / Ira Studio; in **Firozabad** — Abhimanyu Prakash / Siddhivinayak Glass Concepts; in **Goa** — Garima Roy; outside of India — Vanita Varma, Aman Sandhu (for being an impromptu assistant) and Dr. Deepali Dewan / Royal Ontario Museum. We would also like to thank the many people, far and wide, on the streets and in the shops that unknowingly assisted us and provided many glasses of chai and *nimbu pani*. In particular, we thank Prarthna Singh for sharing an aesthetic sensibility and great adventures. We are grateful to Emilia Terragni for enthusiastically taking this project on and to Joe Pickard, Luisa de Miranda and Elizabeth Clinton at Phaidon Press for the various conversations and for coordinating time zones. We are most thankful to our families, particularly our mothers, and the visual language they unknowingly gave us — this book is dedicated to them.

Notes

The following collections, both public and private, allowed us to photograph a number of objects for this book:

Museum of Everyday Art / Sanskriti Foundation: pages 24, 40, 49, 59, 74, 208, 223, 268, 276
Devi Art Foundation: pages 25, 47, 163, 182
Qiyuum Masterji: pages 35, 56, 204
Jalali Heritage House: pages 41, 279
Almond Vilas: page 63
President — Vivanta By Taj: page 66
Anokhi Museum of Hand Printing: page 69
Nira Kehar: pages 71, 127, 277
Sanjay Garg: pages 73, 157, 250-251
Amrapali Jewels: page 85
Wakil Manzil: page 97
Neerja Shah: pages 104, 162, 227, 241
Vechaar Utensils Museum: pages 158, 292
en Inde Trouvée: pages 167, 189, 283
Naheed Carrimjee: page 169
Studio Mumbai Architects / Bijoy Jain: page 179
Serendipity: page 181
Aman Khanna: pages 193, 219
Good Earth: page 199
Anita: page 217
House of MG: page 246
Ankur Tewari: page 253
Fondation d'entreprise Hermès / Khamir: page 267
Thukral & Tagra: page 271
Abode Mumbai: page 275

Phaidon Press Limited
Regent's Wharf
All Saints Street
London N1 9PA

Phaidon Press Inc.
65 Bleecker Street
New York, NY 10012

www.phaidon.com

First published in 2016
© 2016 Phaidon Press Limited

ISBN 978 0 7148 7050 2

A CIP catalogue record for this book is available from
the British Library.

Commissioning Editor: Emilia Terragni
Project Editors: Joe Pickard, Elizabeth Clinton and
Luisa de Miranda
Production Controller: Amanda Mackie
Design by Hyperkit

Photographs by Prarthna Singh, with the exception
of Tiipoi Limited: page 86; Tejas Prithvi: page 93;
Maniyarasan Rajendren: page 165; Yashesh Virkar:
page 174; Erastudio Apartment-Gallery: page 185;
Studio Coppre: page 211; Bernat Camps Parera: page
291; Thukral and Tagra Studio: page 271.

Every reasonable effort has been made to acknowledge
the ownership of copyright for photographs included
in this volume. Any errors that may have occurred are
inadvertent and will be corrected in subsequent editions
provided notification is sent in writing to the publisher.

Printed in China

The publisher would like to thank Jane Birch,
Lise Connellan, Diana LeCore, Kanika Pruthi and
Anna Southgate for their contributions to the book.